HISTORY'S I
A Brief Introd
That Sl

By Arthur J. Amchan

Amchan Publications
7010 Westbury Rd.
McLean, VA 22101

HISTORY'S BARE ESSENTIALS
A Brief Introduction To The Events That Shaped America

By Arthur J. Amchan

Published by:

Amchan Publications
7010 Westbury Rd.
McLean, VA 22101

Library of Congress Control Number: 2012901357
ISBN: 978-0-9617132-5-6

Unless, or until we come up with alternative energy sources that are not prohibitively expensive, dangerous or dirty, the quest for oil will dwarf all other factors in American foreign policy.

Aside from the happy circumstance of the French naval victory that led to Cornwallis' surrender, it is difficult to imagine that England would have ever completely subdued the American rebels.

More than the territorial gains emanating from the Mexican War itself, the conflict is significant in that it upset the status quo with regard to slavery. Southern slave owners were determined to settle the territory gained by conquest and northerners were determined to prevent them from doing so.

Abraham Lincoln never wavered in expressing his conviction that slavery was morally wrong and that he would never agree to its expansion.

World War I changed international relations for the rest of the 20th century and beyond. World War II was essentially a continuation of the First. Moreover, the Cold War Era, which ended in 1991, was a consequence of the First World War.

The highpoint of Reagan's second term was the assistance he lent Gorbachev in destroying Russian Communism.

Prior to the twentieth century (or least since the end of the Crusades), few in the West knew or cared anything about the people and politics of the Arab world or Iran (Persia).

The fall of the Shah of Iran is a turning point in history every bit as significant as the outbreak of World War I, the Communist seizure of power in Russia, or indeed the fall of the Soviet Union and the end of the Cold War.

Unlike certain periods of the past, such as during the Vietnam era, there is little difference between the major American political parties on issues concerning defense and foreign affairs. Both parties are preoccupied with insuring American access to sufficient quantities of petroleum at an acceptable price.

TABLE OF CONTENTS

PREFACE

Fifty-five years or more of reading history and biography led me to write a brief history primer avoiding detail that is unnecessary for readers who are not professional historians, or even self-made experts. I have primarily chosen to cover those events, which I consider most important to contemporary America, including many that occurred overseas.

However, I have also included a few subjects, simply because they strike me as particularly intriguing. An example would be the demonization in the South of Confederate General James Longstreet resulting from his "collaboration" with the post Civil-War Reconstruction Government in Louisiana.

I also stray into short sketches of individuals whose lives I find especially remarkable, such as Andrew Jackson, U.S. Grant, Theodore Roosevelt, Winston Churchill, and several recent American Presidents. I have also briefly summarized the careers of the greatest villains of the twentieth century, Adolph Hitler and Joseph Stalin, because I never cease to be amazed how two seemingly nobodies could come to wield such power and wreck such havoc on humanity.

More briefly I touch upon the careers of certain figures that were far more influential than is commonly recognized. Among these are the German General Erich Ludendorff, who can be held responsible for America's involvement in both world wars and Deng Xiaoping, the Chinese Communist leader who abandoned Marxism and made his country a world power.

I begin with the decision of King Henry VIII of England to break away from the Catholic Church. This ultimately led to the "Glorious Revolution" in 1688, which occurred to insure that all future English monarchs would be Protestants, with somewhat limited powers. The latter event in turn contributed the ideological underpinnings for American Independence and the character of the American Republic.

This book ends with the events occurring as I am writing. A theme of the last part of the book is the extent to which the industrialized world's dependence on oil from the Islamic nations has dominated international relations since the fall of the Soviet Union. I do not cast any moralizing aspersions about this fact because unless, or until we come up with alternative energy sources that are not prohibitively expensive, dangerous or dirty, the quest for oil will dwarf all other factors in American foreign policy.

To understand today's headlines, it is necessary to have some familiarity with the origins of Islam and how events in the Islamic world came to the forefront of Western foreign policy concerns. For example, one cannot possibly understand the Iraq War or the current tensions with Iran without some knowledge of the Sunni-Shiite schism.

Finally, some familiarity with history is essential to understanding both the present and the uncertainties of the future. In this vein, I invoke the line from Shakespeare's *The Tempest,* which adorns the façade of the National Archives in Washington, D.C., "The Past is Prologue."

PART I: The Foundations of the United States:

The Mother Country England becomes Protestant

Independence From England

American History Up to the First World War

The United States is a product of western European culture. More specifically it is part of a culture formed in ancient Greece and Rome, and then nurtured by the Catholic Church for over a thousand years. The United States is predominately Christian because Christianity became the state religion of the Roman Empire in the Fourth Century. It is predominately Protestant because Henry VIII, Elizabeth I and William III made our mother country, England, Protestant. America's culture and political system is derived from England's because the English prevailed over Catholic France in the battle for North America.

England becomes Protestant

The Romans brought Christianity to England. However, the Anglo-Saxons, who invaded the Island after the Romans left, were pagans, who were not converted until the 7th and 8th centuries. The upheaval in

Christendom caused by Martin Luther and Protestantism might have passed the English by were it not for the determination of Henry VIII, starting in about 1525, to divorce his wife and marry his mistress.

Catherine of Aragon, the first of Henry's six wives, was a daughter of the rulers of Spain, Ferdinand and Isabella, possibly the most important monarchs in the history of the West. Her parents' marriage had unified the Spanish kingdoms of Aragon and Castile. Shortly after unification, they conquered the last Muslim stronghold in Spain, Granada, expelled the Jews, started the Inquisition to root out heretics and bankrolled Columbus' first journey across the Atlantic. After Columbus' return, Ferdinand and Isabella and their grandson Charles (Carlos) V sent other Spaniards across the Atlantic to conquer most of South and Central America.

Henry VIII married Catherine in 1509 at about the same time that he became the King. In 1516, Catherine gave birth to a daughter, Mary, later Queen of England from 1553 to 1558 ("Bloody Mary" to Protestants). However, Catherine was unable to produce a male heir. When Henry VIII realized this and once he became enamored with a young lady of the court named Anne Boleyn, he became determined to divorce Catherine.

At first Henry tried to get the Pope to sanction his divorce. Prior to marrying Henry, Catherine was married to Henry's older brother, Arthur, the heir to the English throne. It is doubtful that the marriage was ever consummated since Arthur died in 1502 at the age of 15 after only 20 weeks of marriage.

When Henry decided he wanted to terminate his marriage to Catherine he also decided that the marriage was sinful since Catherine was his brother's widow and that her inability to produce a male heir was due to the fact that the marriage was thus cursed. The Pope, fearful of the reaction of Catherine's nephew, King Charles V of Spain, refused to sanction the divorce. Henry set up his own church and suppressed Catholicism.

Ironically, Anne Boleyn also failed to produce a male heir before Henry had her executed for alleged infidelity and treason. She did produce, however, a daughter in 1533, later Queen Elizabeth I of England from 1558 to 1603, who more than anyone else is responsible for the survival of England as a Protestant nation.

Henry's third wife, Jane Seymour, produced a male heir, who succeeded Henry as Edward VI. However, Edward's death in 1553 at the age of 15 put the survival of Protestantism in England very much in doubt. Protestants at first tried to bring a Protestant cousin of Edward's, Lady Jane Grey, to the throne, but were forced to agree to the rule of Mary Tudor, daughter of Catherine of Aragon and a Catholic.

Mary suppressed Protestantism and married Philip II, King of Spain, and son of her nephew. Fortunately for English Protestants, Mary was unable to bear children. They were also lucky that Mary did not execute her half-sister Elizabeth, who she incarcerated for a time in the Tower of London on suspicion of conspiring with Protestant rebels.

Upon Mary's death in 1558, Elizabeth became Queen, with the support of Phillip II of Spain. Phillip preferred the Protestant Elizabeth to her cousin, the Catholic Mary Queen of Scots, because he feared Mary's ties to his arch-enemy, France, more than Elizabeth's religion. Moreover, for years he retained the hope that Elizabeth would return to the Catholic faith she had feigned while her half sister was alive. This did not happen. As Queen, Elizabeth erased Catholic gains achieved under her half-sister Mary and assured the survival of a Protestant England.

Later in her reign, Elizabeth tried to assist the Dutch Protestants in their efforts to free themselves from the rule of Catholic Spain. She also allowed English mariners to raid Spanish ships laden with treasure from the Americas. In 1588, Phillip II had enough of Elizabeth and sent his fleet towards the British Isles to overthrow her. However, the English fleet and the weather defeated the Spanish Armada.

Elizabeth resisted the pressure put upon her to marry and produce an heir, because she realized that marriage would only diminish her power. She also resisted all efforts to designate an heir to the very end of her life. Finally, she agreed that James VI of Scotland, like herself a direct descendent of her grandfather, Henry VII, would succeed her as James I of England. James was the son of the Catholic Mary Queen of Scots. In 1587 Elizabeth reluctantly executed James' mother, who was her cousin. She did so because Mary was the focus of intrigue by English Catholics and the Spanish to replace Elizabeth as Queen of England. However, James was a Protestant. His accession to the throne in 1603 inaugurated the Stuart dynasty.

Events in 17th Century England lay the foundation for the American Revolution

In 1625, James' son, Charles I became King. Almost immediately a struggle for power began between the King and Parliament, greatly exacerbated by religious overtones. Charles' marriage to a French Catholic made the Protestants suspicious of him. The King's efforts to introduce more pomp and ceremony into Church of England religious practices also made them wary as to whether Charles was gradually turning England back to Catholicism. Many Protestants in Parliament had become more adamant about reducing any similarities between the English Church and Catholicism.

The struggle evolved into civil war, ultimately won by the Parliamentary forces led by Oliver Cromwell. In 1649, the King was tried for treason and executed. Cromwell ruled England afterwards as a military dictator and severely persecuted the Catholics in Ireland. However, after his death and the short reign of his son, Parliament restored the Stuarts to throne of England in the person of Charles II, the deceased King's son. Under Charles II, England was no less of an absolute monarchy than under his father.

Charles II had no legitimate children and upon his death in 1685, his brother, the Duke of York, became King James II. James was a Catholic but had two daughters, later Queen Mary and Queen Anne, who were not raised by him and were Protestant. When James fathered a son by his second wife in 1688, Protestants were sufficiently alarmed by the possibility of a Catholic monarchy that they forced James II to abdicate and leave the country. Parliament replaced James II with his daughter Mary and her Dutch Protestant husband, William of Orange (William III), whom they invited to invade England. This is known as "the Glorious Revolution" and much of the philosophical underpinnings of the American Revolution 88 years later emanate from this period.

William and Mary did not have children, so upon William's death, Mary's sister, Anne, became Queen of England. Anne had a number of children, but none of them survived her. After Anne's son, heir to the throne, died, the English Parliament passed a statute in 1701, which prevented the throne from passing to a Catholic.

As a result when Queen Anne died in 1714, a German prince succeeded Anne as George I. His claim to the throne was based on the fact that he was a great-grandson of James I. George I was the first King of the House of Hanover, to which the current monarch, Elizabeth II, belongs. During World War I the family changed its name to the House of Windsor to remove any questions regarding the family's possible sympathies with Germany.

The Stuarts, however, did not give up the throne of England without a fight. Their supporters, including many Catholics, but also some Protestant Scots, tried to overthrow the House of Hanover. Their objective was to restore James II's Catholic son, James Francis Edward Stuart, and later his grandson (known as "Bonnie Prince Charlie") to the throne. With the support of Spain and later France, the "Jacobites" fought the ruling family on several occasions. "Jacobites" refers to the Latin name for James and has no relationship to the "Jacobins," the radical French revolutionaries. The Jacobites were decisively defeated at Culloden in 1746 by the Hanoverian army.

In 1760, George III, the great-grandson of George I, became King of England at the age of 22. George III came to the throne the year after England's decisive military victories in its imperial war with France in 1759, often called the year of miracles by the English. The most important of these victories was the battle of Quebec, which assured England control of North America. A few years before that, the British East India Company had established its control over the Indian subcontinent. Thus, George III at a tender age became ruler of the most powerful nation on earth.

The struggle for North America

The English had gotten off to a late start in settling the New World. After Columbus, funded by Ferdinand and Isabella, discovered America in 1492, the Spanish quickly began seizing control of much of South and Central America. Columbus' brother established the city of Santo Domingo in 1496. By 1520, the Spanish led by Hernando Cortez conquered the Aztec Empire of Mexico. In 1532, the conquistador Francisco Pizarro conquered the Inca Empire of Peru and several years later founded the city of Lima.

England's first attempt at a permanent settlement in the Americas, Roanoke Island, in what is now North Carolina, was a failure and its residents disappeared without a trace. The second attempt at Jamestown, Virginia in 1607, succeeded, but not by much. The settlers almost starved to death until the arrival of John Smith, who ruled the colony with a heavy hand. The cultivation of tobacco and the introduction of African slavery made the colony economic viable. However, the community came close to being wiped out in 1622, when a Native American uprising killed about a third of the 1,000 settlers.

Nevertheless, the Virginia colony survived and soon other Englishman began coming to America. Charles I's religious policies led a group of Puritan Protestants to leave England and establish Massachusetts Bay Colony. Thousands of English Puritans followed them to New England within a few years. Later in the seventeenth century colonies were established all along the eastern seaboard.

This produced an inevitable confrontation with other colonial powers, most notably France. During the late 17th century, under Louis XIV, France was preoccupied with warfare on the European mainland. Thus, it concentrated on establishing trading posts north and west of the English colonies to obtain valuable furs. France's unwillingness to allow any Protestants to settle in its colonies also limited their growth. The English, by contrast, allowed virtually any Christian to immigrate to its colonies.

By 1734, there were half a million people living in British America, as opposed to about 40,000 in New France. The English settlers began to push west into territory claimed by France. The French were very concerned about this in part because it threatened the link between their colonies in Canada and the colony in New Orleans.

The French began to build forts in what is now western Pennsylvania. An expedition led by 22 year-old George Washington unsuccessfully challenged the erection of these fortifications in 1754. The next year the British sent a large force of British regulars and colonial militia under the command of General Edward Braddock to maintain England's western claims. The twenty-three year-old Washington served as an aide-de-camp to Braddock in this campaign.

Braddock was decisively defeated by the French and their Indian allies in July 1755 and lost his life in the process. The fighting in North America spread to Europe. In the end, Britain emerged victorious. The most important victory was the capture of Quebec City by General James Wolfe in 1759. Although Wolfe did not survive his great victory, it spelled the end of French controlled Canada.

English Victory leads to the American Revolution

The British victory in the French and Indian War planted the seeds for England's loss of its American colonies in the next decade. The tremendous cost of the war made it necessary for the English Parliament to raise revenue. The English thought it perfectly reasonable for the American colonists to pay for a war that in many respects was waged for their benefit.

However, not only did the Americans not enjoy paying additional taxes, they were particularly irked by the fact that the taxes were imposed by a Parliament across the Atlantic Ocean in whose deliberations they had no input. The first direct tax imposed by Parliament, the Stamp Act of 1765, stimulated the first organized opposition to English rule, the Stamp Act Congress.

Another major factor on the road to war was the British Proclamation of 1763. This essentially forbid white settlement west of the Appalachian Mountains. The British government issued the proclamation to buy peace with the western Indians, some of whom had allied themselves with the British against the French. An Indian uprising in the Great Lakes Region led the British to conclude that measures were necessary to placate the Native Americans. To the many colonists, including George Washington, who had invested in land west of the mountains, the proclamation deprived them of opportunity for significant profit. Moreover, to many not so rich colonists, the proclamation squelched their dream of moving west and becoming financially independent landowners themselves.

While revolutions are generally not led by the downtrodden, the American Revolution is somewhat unusual in that its leaders were amongst the most affluent colonists. John Hancock, for example, was one the richest men in Massachusetts. Washington, by marrying the widow Martha Custis, became one of, if not the wealthiest man in Virginia. The American revolutionaries, unlike those later in France and Russia, had no desire to completely overthrow the existing social order.

Another factor in the American Revolution was the influence of the Enlightenment and the philosophical writings of the English "Glorious Revolution" of 1688. First of foremost of these ideas was that the legitimacy of a government stemmed from the consent of the governed, a radical departure from the philosophical principles of most governments, which operated pursuant to the principle of the "divine right of kings."

One should not be a complete cynic and underestimate these principles as a cause of the revolution. The colonists already had considerable experience in self-government and they were determined not to allow the British Parliament or King George III take their right to govern themselves away.

Throughout the late 1760s tension grew between the American colonists and the British Government over the right of the English Parliament to tax Americans. In 1773, a group of colonists protested a new British tax on tea and the monopoly on tea imports that the British Government gave to the British East India Company. They boarded several ships in Boston Harbor dressed as Indians and threw the tea cargo in the water. The British Government, led by Lord North, the Prime Minister, responded by passing several punitive measures, known as the Intolerable Acts.

In response, the colonists, who up to this point were loosely banded together by "Committees of Correspondence," organized the First Continental Congress, which met in Philadelphia in September 1774. The Congress passed resolutions calling for a boycott of British goods if the Intolerable Acts were not repealed and petitioned King George III to redress their grievances. The King, very much under the influence of Lord North, approved an even harder line for dealing with the colonists.

The Second Continental Congress was scheduled to convene in May 1775, again in Philadelphia. By the time the Congress met, hostilities had already broken out between the colonists in Massachusetts and the British. When the British Army decided to march out of Boston in April 1775 to seize weapons and gunpowder stored by the colonists in the town of Concord, the colonial militia mustered to resist.

When the British and Colonials met at Lexington on April 19, 1775, the British ordered the Colonists to disperse. Somebody, nobody knows on which side, fired a shot. Both sides then began shooting. The British quickly scattered the colonials and marched on Concord. However, they were ambushed there and all the way back to Boston by the larger groups of colonials and suffered heavy losses.

Thus, when the Second Continental Congress convened a month later, the Revolutionary War had for all practical purposes already begun. George Washington, a delegate from Virginia, showed up at the Congress in military uniform. Washington had considerable military experience with the British Army during the French and Indian War. Even without the uniform, he was a logical choice to command an army when the Congress authorized its creation. For one thing, as a matter of unity, it was thought wise to give command of the mostly northern army to a southerner.

While Washington was on his way to Boston to assume command of the Continental Army, the British launched an attack on colonial positions overlooking Boston. In the Battle of Bunker Hill, they seized the high ground from the colonists but with such heavy losses, that they made no further attempts at driving the colonials away from the city.

When Washington arrived, he improved the colonial defenses and brought cannons to the heights above Boston, forcing the British to evacuate the city in March 1776. These cannons had been captured earlier by Ethan Allen's "Green Mountain Boys" at Fort Ticonderoga in New York. They were hauled overland under the leadership of Henry Knox, later the artillery commander of the American Army. When the British left Boston, Washington took his army to New York to defend that city from attack.

Independence

Meanwhile, in Philadelphia, the Continental Congress began debating independence from England. Sentiment for independence was by no means unanimous. It was only through the concerted politicking by those favoring the independence resolution, led by John Adams, that the resolution passed on July 2, 1776. On July 4, the Congress adopted the Declaration of Independence, which was drafted by Thomas Jefferson.

In August 1776, the British landed in Manhattan and in a series of battles between August and October 1776, succeeded in driving the Continental Army out of New York City. The British General Sir William Howe nearly trapped Washington's army, but allowed it to escape to New Jersey. Then the British chased the Continental Army through New Jersey into Pennsylvania. However, Washington recrossed the Delaware River and launched a surprise attack on Howe's Hessian mercenaries on Christmas Day 1776 near Trenton, winning a victory that was critical in reviving colonial morale.

In 1851 Emanuel Leutze painted the iconic scene of Washington crossing the Delaware. Behind him holding the flag is Lt. James Monroe, the fifth President of the United States. While Monroe was in fact a veteran of the Battle of Trenton, he most certainly did not cross the Delaware in the same boat as Washington. The famous painting is inaccurate in many other respects, but regardless, it captures the heroism of the moment.

The British Offensives of 1777

The British launched two offensives in the fall of 1777, one aimed at the capture of the colonial capital of Philadelphia, the other at severing the New England states from the rest of the rebellious colonies, by controlling the Hudson River. General Howe sailed from New York and landed his troops near Philadelphia. He then defeated Washington at Brandywine and occupied Philadelphia. The American Congress fled to Lancaster and then York, Pennsylvania.

The British victory was pyrrhic, however. Howe's decision to take Philadelphia, rather then assist General John Burgoyne's army, which was marching south from Montreal, led to a British defeat at the Battle of Saratoga in New York State in October 1777. The victorious American Army at Saratoga was under the command of General Horatio Gates. This led some to call for the replacement of Washington with Gates as Commanding General of the Continental Army.

However, most historians give Gates little credit for the victory. Instead, conventional wisdom is that the American officer most responsible for the victory at Saratoga was Benedict Arnold. Three years later Arnold would defect to the British and become one of the most notorious traitors in history.

The American victory at Saratoga also convinced the French Government of King Louis XVI to openly support the American rebels, although they had been supplying the rebels since the outbreak of the war. Twelve years later the French monarchy would fall to a rebellion in part influenced by the success of the American colonials. However, that was a very different kind of revolution than the one in America.

The entry of France into the American Revolution changed the dynamic of the war fundamentally. The French, unlike the colonials, had a navy comparable to that of England. Fear of the French Navy led General Howe to evacuate Philadelphia in 1778, leaving the British in control of little more than New York City. Then the British turned their attention to the southern colonies. They successfully invaded Georgia where they were encouraged by the number of Loyalists who rallied to the King when they encountered English troops.

The British go south and lose the War

In 1780, the English captured Charleston. However, when the British moved inland, they discovered that Loyalist sentiment was not as widespread as they had hoped. In the southern interior, the American Revolution was a true civil war, with neighbor fighting neighbor. The Americans Patriots dealt the British Army and the loyalist militia a number of defeats in North and South Carolina. Enthusiasm for further prosecution of the war in England began to wane.

However, in some quarters the early British successes in the South encouraged the belief that ultimately the crown would prevail. Benedict Arnold, heretofore one of the greatest American military heroes, decided to cast his lot with the British and sold them the plans to the very strategic American fortress at West Point on the Hudson River.

In exchange, Arnold received money and a commission as a Brigadier General in the British Army. His handler, Major John Andre, aide-de-camp to the British commander in New York City, was to return to the City by ship but was delayed by Arnold's hardball negotiating tactics. Thus Andre had to return by land, was captured out of uniform and was hung by the Americans. Andre's friends in England never forgave Arnold, whom they held responsible for Andre's fate.

In 1781 the British began an offensive in Virginia in which Benedict Arnold played a major role. After initial success, they were checked by Americans under the command of the Marquis de Lafayette, a young French nobleman. Lord Cornwallis, the commander of the British forces in Virginia, was ordered to retreat to Yorktown to await the arrival of a British fleet with reinforcements. After learning that a French fleet was sailing north towards the Chesapeake Bay, Washington and the senior French ground commander, the Marquis de Rochambeau, brought their troops from the north to Virginia and surrounded the British.

A French fleet arrived off Yorktown before the British Caribbean fleet and then drove the British off. Cornwallis was trapped. The Americans and French slowly began their advance on the British lines. One of the final assaults was led by Alexander Hamilton, earlier an aide-de-camp to Washington and later one of the most important players in the establishment of a strong national government.

In October 1781, Cornwallis realizing that he had no hope of being reinforced and that he was about to be overrun by the Americans and French, surrendered to Washington. For all practical purposes, the Revolutionary War was over, although a peace treaty formally ending the war was not signed for another two years. The British did not evacuate New York City until 1783.

Aside from the happy circumstance of the French naval victory that led to Cornwallis' surrender, it is difficult to imagine that England would have ever completely subdued the American rebels. The English could only control the seacoast; the colonials controlled the vast interior of the new United States. Although, it is possible that the outcome of the war might have been something less than full independence, given the decreasing popularity of the war in England and the persistence of the revolutionaries, a return to the status quo was out of the question.

The plight of slaves and Indians in the American Revolution

Although slaves and Indians fought on both sides in the American Revolution, the majority of both groups sided with the British. Many of the Indians realized that a colonial victory would lead to more white settlement west of the Appalachians. The British courted the slaves as Loyalist allies, particularly in the South. The Royal Governor of Virginia, Lord Dunmore, promised freedom to any slave who rallied to the Loyalist cause. In England, the attitude of those unsympathetic with the colonial grievances is best represented by the caustic comment of the writer Samuel Johnson, "How is it that we hear the loudest yelps for liberty among the drivers of Negroes?"

At the end of the war, the British transported many of the slaves who rallied to their side to Canada or their West Indies possessions. Others who fell into the hands of the Patriots were re-enslaved. Prior to the Revolution slavery existed in most Northern states, although over 90% of the American slaves lived in the South. Not too long after the war ended, slavery was abolished in all the northern states.

The Constitution

After several years of independence, it became apparent to many colonial leaders that the national government needed to be strengthened. In 1787 they met at Philadelphia and hammered out the details of a Constitution, which replaced the Articles of Confederation under which the United States Government had been operating.

One major sticking point was the concern of the smaller states about ceding too much power to the larger states. This was resolved by establishing a bicameral legislature. Each state would have 2 senators and a number of representatives based on population. Another sticking point was the interests of the states, such as South Carolina, in which the entire economy and social order was based on African slavery. Despite all the high-sounding rhetoric of the Declaration of Independence, it was obvious that these interests would have to be served if there was to be a federal union.

The Constitution prohibited Congress from banning the importation of slaves until 1808. In determining the number of representatives for each State, the Constitution provided that slaves, who obviously could not vote, counted as 3/5 of a person. In the late 18th century there was some hope that slavery would die out of its own accord due to economic factors. However, the invention of the cotton gin in 1794 made growing cotton much more profitable and markedly increased the economic value of slavery.

With the outlawing of the slave trade in 1808, excess slaves in the Mid-Atlantic States, such as Virginia, became much more valuable. There was less need for them in the areas in which tobacco was the principal crop and a burgeoning need for slave labor in the new lands opening up for cotton cultivation in the Deep South. Thus, much money could be made by slave-owners in states like Virginia, by selling their slaves to plantation owners in the Deep South. Additionally, slave traders got around the prohibition against the slave trade by taking their human cargo from Africa to places like Cuba and then creating falsified records showing that their slaves had been born into slavery in the Central or South America rather than having been born free in Africa.

The more important slavery became to the South, the more aggressive southern politicians became in protecting it in Washington. The nullification crisis of 1830, while facially about a tariff, was in fact a warning shot by southern politicians that the Union would fall apart if the national government did anything to hinder the slave economy.

The Presidency

The new federal Constitution of 1787 also created a strong national executive, the President of the United States. Following the Revolution, there was widespread opposition to creating such an executive given what the colonists considered the high-handed rule by George III. However, it became obvious in the mid-1780s, that if the United States was to be a nation, it needed an executive to make critical decisions. The President's power was curtailed by other provisions of the Constitution requiring the President to share decision-making with the Congress. American history since 1787 has been a constant struggle between the President, Congress and the Supreme Court for power. At times, particularly in wartime, the President has exercised almost dictatorial powers, while at others, such as the period following Watergate, Congress reasserted its authority.

The creation of a strong executive in the Constitution was influenced by the fact that there was only one obvious choice as to who the first President would be. George Washington enjoyed such universal admiration and trust that the Constitution Convention was willing to give him powers that it may have been hesitant to give to others. Washington lived up to his reputation by accepting a second 4-year term only reluctantly and declining a third term. While Washington as a young man appears to have been full of personal ambition, he seems to have outgrown it by the time he reached his mid-50s. Moreover, he had achieved all that one human being could possibly wish to achieve.

The fact that Washington had no children of his own also dispelled fears that the Presidency would evolve into a heredity monarchy. An oddity of American history is that of the first 8 Presidents, only two, John Adams and John Quincy Adams, had male heirs, thus further insuring that the Presidency did not became hereditary.

The early years of the Republic

Washington's administration was characterized by the struggle between his two most prominent cabinet members, Secretary of State Thomas Jefferson and Secretary of Treasury Alexander Hamilton. The two men had very different visions of what their new nation should be. Hamilton was an admirer of England and wished the United States to mimic it in virtually all respects. He wanted a strong national government able to finance itself, close ties to Great Britain and something resembling the British aristocracy.

Ironically, Jefferson, who resembled a British aristocrat far more than Hamilton, envisioned the United States as a basically agricultural country, egalitarian and closely tied to France. The French Revolution took place the same year that Washington took office, 1789. Jefferson and his supporters did not abandon France even while the revolutionaries began executing the nobility, including King Louis XVI and his wife Marie Antoinette.

The French rebels executed many others, including one of the greatest scientists in history, Antoine Lavoisier. Then the revolutionaries began executing each other. The greatest French hero of the American Revolution, the Marquis de Lafayette, barely survived the bloodletting. At various times throughout the early days of the American Republic, the United States came close to war with Britain and France, as each ignored American sensibilities in fighting each other.

The first four U.S. Presidents, Washington, John Adams, Jefferson and James Madison, were each important in the founding of the Republic. Except for Washington, they were far less successful or competent as Chief Executive than they had been prior to their presidencies. While one should be wary of going overboard in historical revisionism, it is important to note that critical assessments of our nation's icons has been engaged in by the icons themselves. For example, Theodore Roosevelt, as a young man wrote a book, "A Naval History of the War of 1812," in which he castigated Jefferson for leaving the United States at the mercy of the British Navy. Jefferson not only opposed the creation of a strong U.S. Navy but also reversed the efforts of John Adams in that regard.

Jefferson's most lasting accomplishment as President was the purchase of the Louisiana Territory, which constitutes one-third of our country (the Mississippi River to the Rocky Mountains) from France. The opportunity for the purchase arose out of domestic developments in France and relations between France and England.

In the late 1790s, as the French Revolution began to run its bloody course, the most successful general of the new French Republic, Napoleon Bonaparte, became the nation's military dictator. In 1804, he crowned himself Emperor of France. Even before becoming Emperor, Napoleon embarked on a series of military campaigns that made him one of the most successful conquerors in all of human history--until he overplayed his hand by invading Russia in 1812.

Napoleon's offer to sell Louisiana to the United States emanated from the failure of a French expedition in 1801 to restore French control over the African slaves and freedmen who had established Haiti as an independent nation. Napoleon then realized that he probably would be unable to defend Louisiana (which he had forced Spain to return to France in 1800) from the British Navy. He thus decided to sell it the United States, rather than lose it to British conquest.

One has to give Jefferson credit for being willing to abandon ideology in purchasing Louisiana. This transaction was contrary to his belief that the Federal Government only had those powers expressly granted to it. The Constitution did not provide explicit authority for the purchase of additional territory.

The War of 1812

America's second war with England began under the most peculiar circumstances. Both England and Napoleonic France were interfering with American shipping as a means to injure each other. Then Napoleon announced to American representatives that France would heretofore respect America's rights as a neutral party. The British foreign minister, George Canning, stupidly refused to do likewise. Thus, the United States Congress declared war on England.

The grievances for which America went to war primarily impacted the coastal states of the Northeast. However, many Americans, particularly in New England were opposed to the war. On the other hand, citizens in the western states were vehemently pro-war. New Englanders realized that the war would only hurt them, since the U.S. Navy, thanks to Jefferson and Madison, was no match for the British Navy operating out of Halifax, Nova Scotia.

The congressmen of the West, such as Henry Clay of Kentucky, viewed the war as an opportunity to conquer Canada and put an end to the Indian threat on the frontier. The westerners believed that England was the prime mover in the Indian uprisings such as that led by Tecumseh, a Shawnee chief, who had united the Indians in what is now Indiana to resist white expansion.

The war went badly for the United States in the Atlantic Ocean and on land. In August 1812, the American garrison at Detroit surrendered to the British and their Indian allies. Although the U.S. Navy won some important moral victories in the Atlantic early in the war, the British Navy was able to blockade all the American ports, with the American frigates at port.

However on the inland lakes, the United States Navy acquitted itself very well. Capt. Oliver Perry's victory on Lake Erie in September 1813 brought English offensives in the northwest to an end. The Americans went on the offensive, during which they burned York, now Toronto. However, the American offensive petered out.

In 1814, the abdication of Napoleon changed the strategic equation dramatically. Now the English could transfer significant armies from Europe to America. However, the British invasion of New York was thwarted by Capt. Thomas MacDonough's victory on Lake Champlain. The British then retreated to Canada.

In the meantime, another British force launched hit and run retaliatory raids along the Atlantic Coast. They temporarily captured Washington,

D.C., sent President Madison running to evade capture and burned the White House and other public buildings in retaliation for the burning of York. Then, they set their sights on Baltimore.

However, at Baltimore, the British failed in their attempt to reduce Fort McHenry, which guarded the entrance to the harbor, and again were forced to retreat. During the British bombardment, an American attorney, Francis Scott Key, wrote a poem, "The Star Spangled Banner," which set to the tune of an old drinking song, became a very popular patriotic hymn. The song officially became the national anthem of the United States in 1931.

Expansion and the slavery question

As slavery became more and more economically profitable due to the invention of the cotton gin, slaveowners became more and more aggressive in defending the institution. They lobbied for legalizing the slave trade and their right to take their slaves with them wherever they settled in the United States.

The first crisis regarding the intertwining issues of slavery and the expansion of the United States occurred in 1819, when Missouri sought statehood. The crisis was averted by the Missouri compromise in which Missouri was admitted to the Union as a slave state, Maine was admitted as a free state and slavery was prohibited in other territories north and west of Missouri. However, since it was obvious that additional states would join the Union, the day of reckoning over slavery had merely been deferred.

Andrew Jackson, the most memorable president between the War of 1812 and the Civil War

The U.S. Presidents between the War of 1812 and the Civil War are generally a forgettable bunch--with the exception of Andrew Jackson, President between 1829 and 1837. Like Theodore Roosevelt seventy years later, Jackson was very good copy both for contemporary journalists and historians. Until recently, he was often rated as one of the greatest Presidents. However, lately his reputation has suffered--in part due to his treatment of the Indians.

It was Jackson who ordered the deportation the agricultural Cherokee Indians from Georgia across the Mississippi River, "The Trail of Tears," during which many died. Jackson's reaction to a Supreme Court decision in favor of the Cherokees was, "[Chief Justice] John Marshall has made his decision, now let him enforce it." However, one must remember that Jackson's attitude towards the Americans Indians was one shared by virtually all white Americans, who wanted Indian land and were willing to use any means, including murder, to acquire it.

Imprisoned on a British prison ship during the Revolutionary War as a teenager, Jackson was the only member of his immediate family to survive the War of Independence. His brother died on the ship and his mother died from disease while treating sick soldiers. Jackson went on to become a lawyer, U.S. Senator and a general in the Tennessee state militia. It was as a military man that he won national recognition, defeating the Indians in Alabama and waging a punitive campaign against the Indians and British agents in Florida. However, it was his victory over British regulars at New Orleans in 1815 that made Jackson a national hero.

Jackson has to be considered the most potentially dangerous man to ever assume the Presidency. Impetuous and prone to violence, it would not have been difficult to imagine Jackson seizing power as a military dictator; however, he did not do so. He peacefully left office after two terms, leaving the country in the hands of his highly competent but very unlucky successor, Martin Van Buren.

The accomplishments of Jackson as president are rather meager. The first years of his administration were dominated by the Peggy Eaton affair. The wives of several other cabinet members, including the wife of Vice President John C. Calhoun, regarded Eaton, the young wife of Jackson's Secretary of War, as little better than a prostitute. Prior to marrying Eaton, Peggy had been married to a man who many believed committed suicide due to Peggy's infidelity.

Jackson considered anyone who failed to accord Peggy Eaton the deference to which he felt she was due, his mortal enemy. This included members of his family as well as former political allies. Jackson's reaction to the treatment of Peggy Eaton may have been due to his enemies' treatment of his wife, who died just before Jackson's inauguration. Rachel Jackson had technically not been divorced from her first husband when she married Andrew. His political opponents labeled Rachel as a bigamist, adulteress and worse.

Andrew Jackson understood next to nothing about economics. One of the greatest issues during his administration was the re-chartering of the Bank of the United States. Jackson's vociferous opposition doomed the Bank and contributed to the depression or Panic of 1837. The other great issue was the nullification crisis, which is the basis for Jackson's reputation, at least until recently, as a great president.

South Carolina, led by Vice President Calhoun, claimed the right to ignore, or "nullify" any federal law with which it did not agree. The crisis arose in the context of tariff that was much more favorable to northern industrial interests than to the agricultural south. However, everyone understood that lurking behind the arguments over principle was the slavery question.

Jackson, although a slave owner and Southerner himself, made it clear that the Federal government was supreme and that he would use force to prove his point. Calhoun backed down, but the tariff was revised more to the liking of the South.

The Mexican War

More than the territorial gains emanating from the Mexican War itself, the conflict is significant in that it upset the status quo with regard to slavery. Southern slave owners were determined to settle the territory gained by conquest and northerners were determined to prevent them from doing so.

As American settlers moved west into Mississippi and Louisiana, it did not take long for them to fix their eyes on the sparsely populated Mexican state of Texas. In 1836, American settlers, after a temporary setback at the Alamo in San Antonio, were successful in gaining independence from Mexico. Southerners quickly began to plan annexation to the United States.

Andrew Jackson's successor, Martin Van Buren, was defeated in the election of 1840 by the Whig candidate, William Henry Harrison. Harrison gained national recognition by his 1812 victory against the Indians at Tippecanoe (not far from the present location of Purdue University in West Lafayette, Indiana). However, he died one month after being inaugurated and was succeeded by John Tyler, a Virginia Democrat, who had bolted to the Whigs for reasons of personal ambition.

The Whigs soon discovered that Tyler was not one of them. One of the respects in which he departed from Whig principles was that he sought congressional approval for the annexation of Texas. Tyler was succeeded as President by Democrat James K. Polk, an Andrew Jackson protégé, who brought Texas into the Union in 1845.

The United States sent an army of observation to Louisiana, whose purpose was to provoke war with Mexico and settle America's boundary dispute with its southern neighbor. In March 1846 General Zachary Taylor crossed the Nueces River which Mexico regarded as the international boundary and engaged the Mexicans.

After a few clashes between the two armies, Taylor crossed the Rio Grande, the boundary claimed by the Americans. President Polk became concerned with General Taylor's popularity and shifted most of his forces to the command of General Winfield Scott at the Mexican port of Vera Cruz.

Scott, imitating the tactics of the conquistador Hernando Cortez, abandoned his supply line at the port and invaded the interior of Mexico. Scott's forces were able to live off the land long enough to capture Mexico City. Among the Scott's staff officers were three who would became very famous in the Civil War, Robert E. Lee, George McClellan and P.G. T. Beauregard.

Playing a far lesser role in the American victory was the quartermaster of the United States Fourth Infantry Regiment, Lt. Ulysses S. Grant. Grant's opinion of the Mexican War, as expressed in the memoir he wrote just before his death in 1886, is as follows:

> The occupation, separation and annexation [of Texas] were, from the inception to the moment of its final consummation, a conspiracy to acquire territory out of which slave states might be formed for the American Union.
>
> ...to this day [I] regard the war as one of the most unjust ever waged by a strong against a weaker nation.

Territorial Gains from the Mexican War upset the status quo

The Mexicans surrendered Mexico City to General Scott in September 1847. Shortly thereafter the United States and Mexico negotiated the Treaty of Guadalupe Hidalgo in which Mexico recognized the Rio Grande as the southern boundary of the United States and ceded what became the States of California, Nevada, Utah, most of New Mexico and Arizona (the rest was purchased in 1852), one third of Texas and parts of Oklahoma, Colorado and Wyoming.

While many argued that the newly acquired territories were unsuitable for slavery, others were not so sure. In August 1846, Congressman David Wilmot of Pennsylvania drew a line in the sand. He introduced a proviso to an appropriations bill specifying that as a condition of acquiring territory from Mexico, slavery would be prohibited in these areas. To many southerners, increasingly both defensive and offensive in protecting their rights to own slaves and to move their "property" anywhere they wished, this was a direct challenge. While the Wilmot Proviso was not adopted by Congress, it set in motion the events leading to the Civil War.

The Road to War: 1850-1861

There are those who minimize and even deny the link between slavery and Civil War. To espouse this view requires either complete ignorance or denial of the events leading up to the War. The best presentation of these events is set forth in Princeton Professor James McPherson's 1989 book *The Battle Cry of Freedom.* McPherson demonstrates how the Civil War was caused by the insistence of southern slaveholders on their right to take their slaves anywhere in the United States.

One of the unfortunate events leading to the Civil War was the death of President Zachary Taylor in July 1850 after less than a year and a half in office. Taylor, although a slaveholder himself, was a strong nationalist. He threatened to use the Army against slaveholders who threatened to defy the federal government regarding the admission of California and New Mexico as free states. Taylor was followed by three of the weakest and worst Presidents in American history: Millard Fillmore, Franklin Pierce and James Buchanan. Each of these couldn't do enough to placate southern slaveholders.

After President Taylor's death, Henry Clay, the leading Whig, and Stephen Douglas, the Democratic leader in the Senate, worked out the Compromise of 1850, which implicitly repealed the Missouri Compromise of 1820, which had outlawed slavery in territory north of the southern boundary of Missouri (although Missouri itself was a slave state). The Compromise of 1850 allowed residents of what is now Utah and Nevada to choose whether or not to allow slavery ("popular sovereignty"). The Compromise also allowed admission of California as a free state but strengthened the fugitive slave law, which enhanced the rights of slaveowners to reclaim slaves who had escaped to free soil.

As another means of protecting their political and economic interests, southerners advocated annexing Cuba as a slave state and also some countries in Central America, where slavery had been abolished. The most notable efforts in this regard were the invasions of Nicaragua by southern private armies, known as filibusters. While the filibusters in Nicaragua gained a temporary success, many there and in Cuba ended up being executed by local, or as in the case of Cuba, Spanish firing squads.

Meanwhile tension increased between the North and South over the fugitive slave laws. In several cases, when southern slaveholders came north to reclaim their escaped "property," they ran into a buzz saw of resistance. One of the most famous instances occurred in Boston in 1854, when a mob of abolitionists attacked the federal courthouse where an escaped slave, Anthony Burns, was being held pending return to his master.

President Pierce called out federal troops to send Burns back to the South--greatly embittering many in the North. This was followed by the Kansas-Nebraska Act in 1854, which explicitly repealed the Missouri Compromise. The architect of this law was Stephen A. Douglas, an Illinois Democrat, with presidential ambitions. At first, Douglas tried to placate the South by drafting a law that would allow residents of Kansas to decide for themselves whether or not to allow slavery--*when Kansas achieved statehood.* However, slaveholders, particularly those in Missouri, who were eyeing Kansas as additional land for their slave-based agricultural enterprises, wanted assurances that they could take their slaves into Kansas while it was still a territory. Douglas accommodated them by redrafting his bill.

The Kansas-Nebraska Act led Abraham Lincoln, a one-time Whig Congressman, to re-enter politics. Campaigning for public office again in 1854, he bitterly denounced the new law and slavery. Today many critics of Lincoln point to statements he made that are by today's standards racist. However, one must consider the popular sentiment in Illinois. If Lincoln espoused racial equality he could not have been elected to anything. However, he made clear his view that the issue of slavery was simply one between right and wrong and he never wavered in his determination to stop its spread.

In 1854 Lincoln was still a Whig and failed to win election to the U.S. Senate [Senators were selected by the state legislatures until the Constitution was amended in 1913 to require selection by the general electorate]. However, the Whig party fell apart over the issue of the extension of slavery. The next year Lincoln joined the new Republican Party, whose primary issue was opposition to the spread of slavery.

The emergence of the Republicans as a viable alternative to the southern-dominated Democratic Party was threatened by the emergence of the American Party, more popularly known as the "Know-Nothings." The Know-Nothings combined opposition to slavery with anti-Catholicism. The emergence of the Know-Nothings was a reaction by American Protestants to the recent immigration of large numbers of Catholics from Ireland and Germany. The former immigrated as a result of the potato famine; the latter as a result of the revolutions in Europe in 1848.

The new arrivals were no more welcome than the Hispanic immigrants, legal and illegal, of today. However, as Samuel Eliot Morison noted in his *History of the American People,* any perspective regarding American anti-Catholicism, should take into account the fact that Catholics in the United States were free to practice their religion, which was not the case for Protestants in Spain and some other Catholic countries.

One of Lincoln's more quotable remarks was his explanation as to why he was not attracted to the Know Nothings.

> As a nation, we began by declaring that all men are created equal. We now practically read it all men are created equal, except Negroes, and foreigners and Catholics. When it comes to this I should prefer emigrating to some country where they make no pretense of loving

liberty--to Russia, for example, where despotism can be taken pure, and without the base alloy of hypocrisy.

Between 1854-1856, a dress rehearsal for the Civil War was waged in Kansas. Slaveholders from Missouri crossed into Kansas territory, the eastern portion of which was no less suitable for slave-holding agriculture than their own state. Opponents of slavery, financed and armed by New England abolitionists also began to settle in the territory.

Kansas territory soon had two competing governments: a free soil government at Topeka and a pro-slavery government at Lecompton. Violence flared both in Kansas and in Washington. Pro-slavery settlers attacked the free-soilers' settlement at Lawrence, Kansas, destroying property but without killing anybody in 1856. However, several free-soilers had been killed elsewhere in the territory. In Congress, South Carolina Congressman Preston Brooks nearly beat Massachusetts Senator Charles Sumner to death with his cane after Sumner concluded a speech attacking the pro-slavery forces in Kansas and their supporters in Congress.

The attack on Lawrence, the murder of free soilers and the caning of Charles Sumner greatly inflamed 56 year-old John Brown, an abolitionist zealot, who had come to Kansas to join six of his sons. In May 1856, Brown and four of his sons and other followers murdered five pro-slavery settlers in cold blood. This sparked an enhanced shooting war between the free-soilers and slave-holding settlers.

In 1857 pro-slavery settlers approved a constitution at Lecompton and petitioned Congress for admission to the Union as a slave state. A competing petition was submitted by free-soilers who by this time clearly were a majority in Kansas territory. The new President, James Buchanan, caved into southern pressure and recommended admission of Kansas to the Union as a slave state. This was too much for Stephen A. Douglas, the odds-on favorite to be the Democratic presidential nominee in 1860.

Douglas had tried to finesse the slavery issue with the concept of "popular sovereignty." He recognized that admission of Kansas as a slave state violated that principle and would destroy the Democratic Party in the North. He refused to support admission of Kansas as a slave state without a popular referendum. By doing so, he alienated the South and lost whatever chance he had of becoming president.

The Dred Scott decision

In 1846, on the advice of white advisors, Dred Scott, a slave in St. Louis, filed suit claiming that the several years he had spent in free territory made him a free man. In 1856, his case made it to the United States Supreme Court. In 1857, one month after the inauguration of President Buchanan, the southern dominated Court, in an extremely inflammatory opinion written by the Chief Justice, Roger B. Taney, ruled against Scott. Taney went far beyond what was necessary to decide the case.

Taney opined that the Declaration of Independence did not apply to Negroes and "that they had no rights which a white man was bound to respect." The Court ruled that the Missouri Compromise of 1820 was unconstitutional because Congress had no authority to prohibit slavery in the territories. This undercut Stephen Douglas' argument to northerners that the slavery issue could be finessed by "popular sovereignty."

Douglas, before and during his famous debates with Lincoln in 1858, argued that slavery could still be banned in the territories by failing to pass laws to enforce the slaveholders' rights. Southerners responded by insisting that such laws be passed and enforced. Lincoln, for his part, argued that the *Dred Scott* decision by implication meant that Congress did not have the authority to prohibit slavery anywhere. The slaveholders, he warned, would not be satisfied until all the states of the Union were made hospitable to slavery.

Although the Illinois legislature re-elected Douglas to the United States Senate, the seven debates between Lincoln and Douglas in 1858 made Lincoln a national figure, in large part because of the identity of his opponent. Douglas appealed to the basest racist fears, arguing that if the Republicans came to power white women would be forced to marry black men. Lincoln, although on the defensive on "racial mixing," never wavered from the proposition that Negroes were human beings, not simply "property" as the slaveholders contended. He publicly proclaimed that blacks were entitled all the rights enumerated the Declaration of Independence: life, liberty and the pursuit of happiness.

Many historians have cited an 1862 letter Lincoln wrote to Horace Greeley as evidence that he was indifferent to the plight of the slaves. In that letter, Lincoln wrote that if he could save the Union without freeing any slaves he would do so. However, to take this statement out of the context of all the things Lincoln said on the subject is a mistake. He never wavered in expressing his conviction that slavery was morally wrong and that he would never agree to its expansion. Although he was skeptical that whites and free blacks in significant numbers could live together in the United States, he made it clear that Negroes had many rights that whites were bound to respect.

The next great watershed on the road to war occurred in October 1859. John Brown, now 60, and financed by six New England abolitionists, attacked the Federal Arsenal at Harper's Ferry, (now West) Virginia. His plan was to distribute weapons from the arsenal to slaves in the area and start a full-blown slave insurrection. After taking the arsenal, Brown stayed put. No slaves came to join his band, but state militia troops and U.S. Marines under the command of Army Col. Robert E. Lee and Lt. J.E.B. Stuart arrived very quickly.

Brown's raid was a fiasco, but he salvaged his reputation with an eloquent speech at his trial. Brown was hung in Charleston, Virginia in December 1859 and on the basis of his farewell speech became an instant martyr in the North. More than Brown's raid, the northern reaction to it convinced many in the South that a substantial number of the northerners would not be satisfied unless their slaves slaughtered them.

Southerners had good reason to fear a slave insurrection. There had been several such uprisings in the 18th century, including one in New York in 1741. In the 19th century, the most notable were ones led in 1822 by a slave named Denmark Vesey in Charleston, South Carolina, which was aborted and the 1831 Nat Turner rebellion in Tidewater Virginia. Fifty five to sixty five whites were killed in the Turner uprising. Curiously, there were no major slave insurrections during the Civil War, when most white men were away from the plantations serving in the Confederate Army.

The Presidential Nominating Conventions of 1860

There were two Democratic Party nominating conventions in 1860, the first at Charleston, and the second at Baltimore. Most southerners were determined to make Stephen Douglas pay for his apostasy in failing to fully support the slaveholders in Kansas. They nominated Buchanan's Vice-President, John C. Breckinridge, for President. Douglas won the nomination from the rest of the party, but the split made it quite likely that the Republicans, running a presidential candidate for only the second time, would capture the presidency.

The Republicans met in Chicago, which greatly improved the chances of Illinois' favorite son, Lincoln, to win the nomination. Lincoln was also helped by the perception that he was a less polarizing candidate than the better-known William H. Seward. However, politicians from the Deep South made it clear that a victory by any Republican would lead them to secede from the Union.

The election of 1860 leads the cotton states to secede

Lincoln triumphed in a four-way race. He carried most of the North; Breckinridge carried the Deep South and John Bell, the candidate of the Constitutional Union Party, carried Virginia, Kentucky and Tennessee. Bell's party's platform was to make believe a crisis did not exist. Although Stephen Douglas received the second greatest number of popular votes, he received only 12 electoral votes. Had Douglas been elected, his presidency would have been very short. After pleading with the country to accept the election of Lincoln, he died in June 1861 at the age of 48.

The Deep South slaveholders were good to their word. Upon learning of the election results, South Carolina called a convention, which unanimously enacted an ordinance of secession on December 20, 1860. The rest of the lower South; Mississippi, Florida, Alabama, Georgia, Louisiana and Texas followed suit well before Lincoln's inauguration on March 4, 1861. The other slave states adopted a wait and see attitude.

Representatives of the secessionist states met in Montgomery, Alabama and adopted a constitution for the Confederate States of America. The delegates elected Jefferson Davis, a Mississippi Senator, former Secretary of War and Mexican War hero, as President. Almost immediately, a crisis arose over the fate of federal property in the Confederacy. The attention of both sides focused on Ft. Sumter in the middle of Charleston harbor.

Buchanan, pressured by several unionist democrats who had recently joined his administration, refused to turn Ft. Sumter over to the South Carolinians. Buchanan even authorized an unsuccessful attempt to reinforce and resupply Ft. Sumter in January 1861. When Lincoln took office on March 4, the garrison at Sumter was running out of supplies. Thus, Lincoln was faced with the choice of surrendering Fort Sumter or risking war. He chose the latter.

Civil War

Lincoln notified the Governor of South Carolina that he would resupply Fort Sumter but would not send reinforcements or additional weapons. The Confederate Government in Alabama ordered its commander, P.G.T. Beauregard, to reduce the Fort before the relief expedition arrived. On April 12, the Confederates opened fire. Thirty three hours later the garrison surrendered.

Three days later, Lincoln called for 75,000 volunteers to suppress the rebellion. War fever swept both North and South and Civil War was a reality. Lincoln's call to arms also pushed a number of the Upper South States: Virginia, North Carolina and Tennessee into the Confederacy. Only quick action by union supporters in Maryland and Kentucky prevented those states from also throwing in their lot with secession.

In Missouri, Capt. Nathaniel Lyon saved the state for the Union by organizing ethnic German unionists into an armed force and chasing the secessionists into the southwest corner of the state. Unwilling to retreat in the face of a superior Confederate force, Lyon, by then a General, was killed near Springfield, Missouri in August 1861.

In July the Union Army under the command of General Irwin McDowell engaged the Confederates near Manassas, Virginia and was defeated, sending shockwaves through the North and reinforcing the southern view that the Federal Army was a paper tiger.[1] Lincoln then appointed George B. McClellan to be commander of Union forces in the East. McClellan, who rejoined the army after a successful career as a railroad executive, became a national hero by defeating the Confederates in western Virginia and keeping open the railroad route between Ohio and Virginia. McClellan devised a plan to capture Richmond by landing his troops at Yorktown, Virginia and marching them westward to the new Confederate capital via the peninsula formed by the York and James Rivers.

---

[1] Civil War battles were often referred to by the name of the closest town by the South (i.e., Manassas), but

In the spring of 1862, McClellan reached the gates of Richmond, but the Confederates, under the command of Robert E. Lee and Thomas "Stonewall" Jackson defeated him in a series of battles in May forcing McClellan to retreat. General John Pope, who had achieved some modest success against Confederate forces in the West, attacked the Confederates at Manassas again in August 1862 and was soundly defeated. The Union armies in the East were then consolidated again under General McClellan, who was now confronted with Lee's first invasion of the North.

In September 1862, McClellan, aided by a copy of Lee's orders, which fell mysteriously into his hands, checked the Confederate invasion at Antietam Creek near Sharpsburg, Maryland. However, much to Lincoln's chagrin, McClellan did not pursue Lee and allowed him to cross the Potomac River to safety. Lincoln's unhappiness with his commander did not stop him from taking advantage of the "victory" to issue the Emancipation Proclamation liberating all the slaves in Confederate, but not Union territory.

The Emancipation proclamation was a major change in policy by the Lincoln administration. In May 1861, General Benjamin Franklin Butler, in command at Ft. Monroe, Virginia had refused to return slaves who had sought refuge at the fort, to their Confederate owners. The initial refugees had been building fortifications for the Rebels, so Butler, reasoning that this situation was no different than intercepting weapons bound for the Confederates, declared the Negroes "contraband of war." However, he and other Union commanders began refusing to return slaves who had not been actively put to use in the Rebel war effort.

In August 1861, General John Fremont, who had been the first Republican presidential candidate in 1856, declared all the slaves owned by Confederate activists in Missouri to be free. Lincoln countermanded Fremont's order for fear of driving border states like Kentucky and Maryland into the arms of the Confederacy.

By mid-1862, Lincoln was increasingly concerned with the possibility that England and France would recognize the independence of the Confederacy. Additionally, as the war dragged on, more people in the North came to view the slaves as an asset to the Confederate war effort and the underlying cause of the war.

Thus after Antietam, to discourage the Europeans powers from recognizing the Confederacy and to deprive the Rebels of slave labor, Lincoln proclaimed that come January 1, 1863, all slaves in those areas in rebellion against the United States would be free. Although the Emancipation Proclamation said nothing about slaves living in the border states or southern areas under the control of the Union Army, it was generally understood that the Proclamation would lead to the demise of slavery throughout the United States.

Following Antietam, Lincoln again became tired of General McClellan's reluctance to engage the enemy and fired him. His replacement as Commanding General of the Army of the Potomac, Ambrose Burnside, quickly demonstrated his incompetence by attacking Confederate positions at Fredericksburg in December 1862, only after giving Lee weeks to make them impregnable.

Lincoln replaced Burnside with General Joseph Hooker, to whom he wrote a classic letter concerning rumors about Hooker's reputed desire to become a military dictator. Lincoln essentially told Hooker that if the General could produce victories, he would chance the dictatorship.

However, Hooker did not bring victory, but instead brought a disastrous defeat at Chancellorsville in May 1863. Lee followed up this victory by invading the North again. His invasion was checked by the Army of the Potomac under the command of George Meade in the largest battle of the war at Gettysburg, Pennsylvania July 1-3, 1863. However, like McClellan at Antietam, Meade allowed Lee to escape to Virginia across the Potomac.

Although, the battles in East were not going well for the Union, progress in the West was much more satisfactory. From the western theatre emerged the greatest military hero in American history, Ulysses S. Grant, one of the unlikeliest people to save his country.

U. S. Grant

No historical figure's life is more inspirational than that of Grant. While George McClellan was a man with many credentials, he was a failure in the great tasks entrusted to him. Grant, a man with little in the way of credentials, succeeded.

Grant graduated from West Point where he excelled only in his ability to handle horses. He served honorably and bravely in the Mexican War as a regimental quartermaster. However, in 1852 he resigned from the Army, most likely due to alcoholism. In the next 8 years he met nothing but failure. The outbreak of the Civil War found Grant working in a store in Galena, Illinois owned by his father and run by his younger brothers.

Since few in the North had any military experience and competent commanders for the millions now bearing arms were hard to come by, Grant was appointed commanding officer of an Illinois regiment. Almost immediately, he began winning battles and was awarded larger commands. His victories at Fort Henry and Fort Donelson on the Tennessee and Cumberland Rivers in February 1862 brought him national attention.

After narrowly avoiding defeat at Shiloh in April 1862, also on the Tennessee River, and being temporarily sacked, Grant began waging a campaign to secure the Mississippi River for the Union in the fall of 1862. In this campaign, he and his principal subordinate, General William Tecumseh Sherman, were innovative. At one point, they tried to bypass the Confederate stronghold at Vicksburg, Mississippi, by building canals around it. Failing at that, Grant laid siege to the city, which surrendered to him on July 3, 1863, the same day that Union forces at Gettysburg repelled Lee's frontal assault on their lines.

In November 1863, Grant commanded victories at Missionary Ridge and Lookout Mountain near Chattanooga, Tennessee and began preparing to advance on the strategic Confederate rail junction at Atlanta, Georgia. Despite southern victories in the East, Grant had cut the heart out of the Confederacy. At this point, Lincoln called him to Washington, promoted Grant to Lt. General, a rank previously held only by George Washington, and appointed him General in Chief of the Union Armies.

Rather than return to the Atlanta campaign, Grant decided to stay in Virginia and leave Sherman responsible for the drive on Atlanta. Although General Meade was nominally in command of the Army of the Potomac, Grant made all the strategic decisions.

Grant first engaged Lee's Army of Northern Virginia in the Wilderness on May 5, 1864, not far from the sites of the 1862 Battle of

Fredericksburg and the 1863 Battle of Chancellorsville. In his first engagement with the eastern Confederates Grant was beaten as badly as Burnside and Hooker before him. The difference was that he did not flinch and head back towards Washington. He tracked Lee's Army heading southeast and attacked again the next week at Spotsylvania and a month later at Cold Harbor. On both occasions Grant failed to win a significant victory while sustaining fearsome casualties. His detractors labeled Grant a butcher, but Grant was determined to win the war and take chances to do it.

Grant crossed the James River and forced Lee into a defensive posture around Richmond. In July 1864, only malfeasance by a regimental commander deprived him of the critical victory south of Richmond. Coal miners in the Union ranks tunneled under the Confederate fortifications and blew a huge hole in the Rebel lines. However, the Colonel of the lead attacking regiment was drunk and failed to exploit the opening. Then the war settled down to trench warfare. Grant kept moving his lines westward to encircle Lee. In this effort he employed large numbers of black soldiers, the U.S. Colored Troops.

In the summer of 1864 the war appeared to be stalemated again causing Lincoln to believe that he would be defeated in the November presidential election. However, early in the fall the Union won two significant victories that contributed greatly to his re-election over the Democratic candidate George B. McClellan. On September 2, Atlanta fell to General Sherman and in October, Philip Sheridan decisively defeated the Confederates in the Shenandoah Valley of Virginia.

As a measure to unify the country, the Republicans replaced Vice-President Hannibal Hamlin with the Democratic War Governor of Tennessee, former U.S. Senator Andrew Johnson. Lincoln's re-election guaranteed that the Union would prosecute the war to total victory.

In April 1865, Grant succeeded in flanking Lee's fortifications and the Confederate commander was forced to abandon Richmond. Running battles continued as Lee moved west. Finally, the Union Army got between Lee and his supply line to North Carolina. Lee surrendered the Army of Northern Virginia to Grant on April 9, 1865 at Appomattox Court House.

The Civil War did not end at Appomattox. Several other Confederate Armies were still in the field. Later in April, Confederate General Joseph E.

Johnston surrendered to General Sherman in North Carolina. It was not until May that the last major Confederate Army surrendered in Texas. Nevertheless, U.S. Grant emerged from the Civil War as the greatest American hero since Washington. Unfortunately, his historical reputation was greatly diminished by his Presidency between 1869 and 1877.

Sherman's March to the Sea

While Grant was shadowing Lee in Virginia, his lieutenant, William Tecumseh Sherman was ripping the heart out of the rest of the Confederacy. After taking Atlanta, Sherman replicated Winfield Scott's march on Mexico City by cutting loose from his supply lines and heading towards the Atlantic Ocean to Savannah, which he reached by Christmas. The Confederates thinking Sherman would be obliged to follow them, moved back into Tennessee where they were defeated by George Thomas at Nashville in December 1864.

In Georgia, Sherman's army left a path of destruction in its wake, but more serious plundering began as his Army turned north and entered South Carolina. Sherman, holding that state responsible for the outbreak of the war, essentially gave his men free rein in destroying or stealing everything in sight. His march devastated Columbia, South Carolina, but spared Charleston, which withstood several full-scale assaults by the Union Army and Navy.

The assassination of Abraham Lincoln and the consequences of the Civil War.

On April 14, 1865, John Wilkes Booth, a prominent actor and Confederate sympathizer, assassinated Abraham Lincoln while the President attended a play at Ford's Theater in Washington, D.C. The new President, Andrew Johnson, clashed with the "Radical Republicans" over what to do with the conquered South. A major source of disagreement was the relationship between the freed slaves and the whites. Johnson was far less interested in protecting Negroes than were many of the Congressional Republicans and Edwin Stanton, who he had inherited as Secretary of War from Lincoln.

In 1868 there was a showdown between Johnson and the Republican leadership when Johnson attempted to remove Stanton from office. The

House of Representatives voted to impeach Johnson, but the Senate failed by one vote to remove him from office. Soon thereafter, Johnson was succeeded as President by General Grant.

Along with Warren Harding's in the 20th century, Grant's presidency was most notable for its corruption. In recent times, some historians have attempted to rehabilitate Grant's reputation as President by arguing that he was the last President to attempt to protect the freed slaves. This attempt does not withstand close scrutiny as much of the Republican rhetoric about the Negroes in the South was merely posturing.

"The tragic era:" America returns to its racist roots

For a brief period of time at the end of the Civil War and for a few years thereafter, a majority, or at least a substantial minority of Northerners seemed to come around to the Radical Republican view that blacks were entitled to the same civil rights as whites -- at least if they stayed in the South. The Federal Government established the Freedman's Bureau to assist the ex-slaves in their transition to freedom. Federal troops were stationed in the former Confederate states to assist in this effort.

Congress passed the Reconstruction Acts in 1867, which placed the South under military rule and fostered the development of state governments run by blacks, and whites considered loyal to the national government. Many of the whites were union soldiers who had settled in the South after the war, labeled "carpetbaggers" by the unreconstructed white southerners. Southern whites that either opposed secession or repudiated it were labeled "Scalawags."

The most notable scalawag was the General James Longstreet, possibly the most prominent Confederate war hero to survive the conflict except for Robert E. Lee. At the Second Battle of Bull Run, Chickamauga and the Wilderness, it was the appearance of Longstreet's Corps that turned the tide in favor of the Confederates. At the Wilderness, he was nearly mortally wounded when mistakenly fired upon by Confederate soldiers.

After the war, however, Longstreet not only advocated accommodation with the Reconstruction Acts, he served as adjutant general and later commander of the Louisiana state militia during Reconstruction. He commanded this militia in its unsuccessful battles with white supremacists in 1874. As a result of his post-war activities it became accepted as gospel in the South that Lee's defeat at Gettysburg was due to insubordination and even treason on the part of Longstreet.

While schools, streets, parks and military installations throughout the South were named for other Confederate heroes, none, or few, bear the name of General James Longstreet. The charges against Longstreet were politically motivated lies. Lee, who died in 1870 before Longstreet's enemies revised the history of the battle of Gettysburg, had plenty of opportunities to relieve Longstreet of his command and never did so, as he did with others. It defies credulity that Lee would retain as his principal corps commander a man he suspected of disloyalty or insubordination in one of the most important junctures of the war.

By 1876, northern interest in protecting southern blacks from southern whites had run its course. The last act of reconstruction was the removal of federal troops from South Carolina. This was likely the result of a deal between the Republican candidate for President, Rutherford B. Hayes, a union veteran, and Wade Hampton, a former Lt. General in Confederate Army. In exchange for the removal of federal troops and Hampton's acquiescence to his becoming President, Hayes acquiesced in Hampton becoming the Governor. Although, some historians have accused Hayes of selling the southern blacks out, he had little choice because there was no support in the North for restarting the Civil War to prevent the former Confederates from regaining political control of their states.

In 1883, the United States Supreme Court, the majority of which had been appointed by Republican presidents, declared the Civil Rights Act of 1875 unconstitutional. That statute had required equal enjoyment of public accommodations. The court concluded that the Fourteenth Amendment to the Constitution, enacted after the Civil War, only forbade discriminatory state action, not private acts of discrimination. The decision was an open invitation to white southerners to use subterfuge to undo all the vestiges of Reconstruction.

The lone dissenting justice was John Marshall Harlan of Kentucky. Ironically, Harlan, although a Union Army veteran, had bitterly opposed emancipation of the slaves and the post-war amendments to the Constitution that had been adopted to protect the freed slaves from their neighbors. Once converted to the cause of Negro political and civil rights, Harlan was the freedman's lonely champion on the court throughout his 34 years of service.

Harlan noted that innkeepers and other operators of public accommodations needed state approval to run their businesses. He wondered why the court had such a difficult time prohibiting private discrimination. Before the Civil War, the Court had no trouble sustaining legislation, such as the Fugitive Slave Act, that prohibited private action to protect the slaves.

In 1890 Mississippi became the first state to virtually eliminate black voting through amendments to the state constitution. In the same year, "Pitchfork" Benjamin Tillman, a virulent racist, defeated the aristocratic faction of Wade Hampton and assumed leadership of the Democratic Party of South Carolina. Running for re-election in 1892, Tillman advocated the lynching of any black charged with raping a white woman. In 1895, he engineered a new state constitution effectively disenfranchising South Carolina's Negroes. The other former Confederate states followed suit in making it virtually impossible for blacks to vote anywhere in the South.

The State of Louisiana passed a law in 1890 requiring railroad accommodations in the state to be segregated. Black citizens challenged the law, which was upheld by the United States Supreme Court in *Plessy v. Ferguson* in 1896, with only Justice Harlan dissenting. The *Plessy* decision was deemed so unremarkable that Charles Warren's monumental *The Supreme Court in United States History* written in the 1920s did not even mention it.

In 1901 President Theodore Roosevelt invited Booker T. Washington, regarded as the spokesman for all American Negroes, to dinner at the White House. Washington preached self-improvement and resignation to existing racial attitudes. During the Civil Rights era his reputation suffered greatly. Blacks generally regarded him as an enabler of racial segregation.

Benjamin Tillman, then a Senator from South Carolina, stated that thousands of blacks would have to be killed to put them back in their place as the result of President Roosevelt's dining with Booker T. Washington. While the President reacted with defiance, one of his admirers, the prominent historian James Ford Rhodes wrote:

> [His] mature opinion afterwards was different. He said to me that he had made a mistake in asking Booker Washington to dinner; that among Southerners there was prejudice against such action and, while he could not comprehend their feeling, it was there and had to be reckoned with...It was understood that he did not approve of the policy of forcing Negro suffrage upon the Southern States...involved in the Reconstruction Acts of Congress and the XV amendment, and he never repeated the Booker Washington incident. In his autobiography written in 1913 he made no mention of it.

Neither Rhodes' views nor the President's was inconsistent with the prevailing view. Many, but not all of the most vocal defenders of the freed slaves lost interest in them, and some like the Reconstruction Governor of South Carolina, Daniel Chamberlain, became white supremacists. The Democrats of the early 20th century, still the party of the white south, were worse than the Republicans, who merely postured on behalf on blacks. Democrat Woodrow Wilson imposed racial segregation in government offices in which it had not previously existed.

One of the most popular books of the late 1920s and 1930s was *The Tragic Era* by Claude Bowers, which depicted Reconstruction as a crime committed against white southerners. Bowers' book was consistent with the prevailing view of the Reconstruction period. This changed dramatically after the Civil Rights era.

Beyond this there were many whites that continued to reject the idea that blacks had any rights, which a white man was bound to respect. A good expression of this view is found in the biography of the Confederate General Nathan Bedford Forrest, written by Dr. John Allan Wyeth, a Confederate veteran and later President of the American Medical Association. In *That Devil Forrest,* written in 1899, Dr. Wyeth observed:

> In the crisis of a great civil war... the leaders of the opposing forces justified a resort to measures of diplomacy in order to weaken their antagonists, which a strict construction of right and truth would not have allowed. The proclamation of emancipation may be mentioned as such a measure-the unlawful and unjust sweeping away of private property.

The closing episodes of the Indian Wars

The United States Army in 1898 consisted of only 28,000 regular soldiers. Between the Civil War and the Spanish War, the job of the Army was almost exclusively protecting white settlers in the western United States from the Indians. The most memorable episode of the confrontations between the Army and the Indians occurred in June 1876, when the Civil War hero, George Armstrong Custer and five companies (or troops) of the 7th Cavalry Regiment were wiped out at the Battle of the Little Big Horn in Montana.

Another famous episode of the U.S. Army's campaigns against the Indians was the pursuit of the Apache warrior Geronimo and his followers, who wrecked havoc and terror amongst white settlers in Arizona before surrendering to General Nelson Miles in 1886. The last major episode of the Indian Wars was the incident at Wounded Knee in South Dakota in 1890, often called the Wounded Knee Massacre. The killing at Wounded Knee was not premeditated. Soldiers from the Seventh Cavalry intended to force a band of Sioux back to the reservation without violence.

This band of Sioux was among thousands of Indians in the West who left their reservations during the "Ghost Dance Crisis." Many Indians came to believe that participation in the Ghost Dance ceremony would issue in a messianic era in which the white men would disappear and they would be able to resume a nomadic lifestyle hunting big game.

At Wounded Knee, when the soldiers attempted to disarm the Indians, an unanticipated firefight broke out with casualties on both sides. Then the soldiers began firing indiscriminately, killing an estimated 150-300 Indians including many women and children. 25 soldiers were killed and 35 were wounded in the fight.

The War with Spain in 1898: America becomes a player in international affairs

Before the Civil War, Southerners cast their eyes on Cuba as a potential slave state. After the Civil War, America's interest in acquiring the Island or at least effective control over it continued. Spain, greatly weakened by the independence of most of its other American colonies earlier in the 19th century, was no longer a world power with which the United States needed to be seriously concerned.

In 1868, a rebellion against Spanish rule broke out in the Island. Many in Congress wanted to intervene on the side of the rebels and President Grant attempted unsuccessfully to negotiate the acquisition of Cuba by the United States. The Cuban rebellion continued and the Spanish Government resorted to harsh measures to suppress it.

In 1897, a more liberal Spanish Government in Madrid replaced the Governor General with a more benign officer. Hard-liners in the Spanish military rioted in Havana. On the advice of the American counsel in Havana, the former Confederate General Fitzhugh Lee, President McKinley dispatched the battleship Maine to Havana to protect American nationals.

Several weeks later the Maine exploded in Havana harbor killing 262 American sailors. Although no hard evidence linked the Spanish to the tragedy, public opinion led President McKinley to seek a declaration of war. On February 25, 1898, the Assistant Secretary of the Navy, Theodore Roosevelt, itching for opportunities for martial glory, wired the American naval commander in the Far East, Commodore George Dewey, to prepare for offensive operations in the Philippine Islands.

On May 1, 1898, Dewey steamed into Manila Bay and destroyed the Spanish Pacific fleet without losing a man. In June and July, ground troops under the command of Major-General Wesley Merritt, a union cavalry commander in the Civil War, went into action. The Spanish, having no hopes of reinforcement or resupply, fought just enough to satisfy their concepts of honor and then surrendered on August 13.

The small size of the regular Army led President McKinley to call for 125,000 volunteers to combat the Spaniards. This presented the President, a union veteran, the opportunity to solidify the reunification of the country by commissioning a number of Confederate veterans to commands in the U.S. Volunteers. Most notable of these appointments was that of Joseph Wheeler, a Democratic Congressman, to the command of the U.S. cavalry in Cuba.

In his younger day, Wheeler had been a famous commander of Confederate cavalry in Tennessee, Kentucky and Georgia. It was Wheeler who was given principal responsibility for stopping Sherman's march to the Sea in 1864. His lack of success was due to the paucity of men he had to accomplish this task.

After the declaration of war in April 1898, the Fifth Army Corps assembled at Tampa, Florida under the command of General William R. Shafter, an obese Union Civil War hero, who like many of the top commanders was in his sixties. Among the regiments in the Fifth Corps was the First Volunteer Cavalry Regiment, better known as the "Rough Riders," commanded by Colonel Leonard Wood. Wood's second in command was Lt. Col. Theodore Roosevelt, who had resigned as Assistant Secretary of the Navy to seek glory in armed combat.

The Fifth Corps landed in Cuba in June 1898 and advanced to the base of San Juan Heights, which constituted the last line of defense for the Spanish soldiers protecting the city of Santiago in whose harbor the Spanish Caribbean fleet was trapped. On the morning of July 1, Spanish troops opened fire on the Americans who then assaulted the heights. Although regular army infantry units played the major role in the capture of the heights, most of the publicity went to Teddy Roosevelt, who had become the regimental commander of the "Rough Riders."

Roosevelt, possibly the greatest self-promoter in American history, and possibly the best media personality this country ever produced, did much to enhance the impression that he played a more vital role in the successful assault than he in fact did. The satirist Peter Finley Dunne, (aka "Mr. Dooley,") suggested that Roosevelt should have entitled his war memoirs, "Alone in Cuba."

After the capture of the Heights, the Army and Navy could not agree upon which should assault Santiago. Yellow Fever broke out among the U.S. forces and General Shafter considered withdrawing from the heights. Fortunately for the Americans, the Spanish fleet attempted to break out of Santiago harbor and was wiped out by a U.S. Naval Squadron, which suffered virtually no losses. Like their compatriots in the Philippines, the Spanish garrison had no hope of being reinforced or resupplied. It quickly surrendered and the Army invaded Puerto Rico, the only remaining Spanish colony in western hemisphere, which was subdued virtually without any fighting.

Fallout from the Spanish War

The United States now wrestled with what to do with the former Spanish colonies. Cuba became an independent country--with strings attached. In 1903 Congress passed the Platt Amendment, which required the Cuban Government to allow American intervention in Cuba's domestic affairs whenever the United States deemed it necessary. It also required Cuba to lease to the United States the naval station at Guantanamo Bay, which the U.S. Navy maintains to the present day. This facility now hosts many prisoners captured in the aftermath of 2001 attacks on the United States.

Puerto Rico and the Philippines became U.S. territories. However, to maintain control of the latter, the United States fought a three-year war with Filipino nationalists, 1899-1902, in which 70,000 Americans served and 4,000 died. Afterwards, the insurrection continued in the Muslim areas of the Island of Mindanao for several years. Capt. John J. Pershing, later commander of the American expeditionary force in World War I, enhanced his reputation during this period by subduing the "Moros." Not until 1946 did the Philippines become completely independent of the United States.

Theodore Roosevelt

One of the best-known American Presidents is Theodore Roosevelt (TR). This is somewhat curious in that he occupied the White House in relatively uneventful years. However, he thrust the Federal Government into management of the American economic system to a greater extent than any previous peacetime president. He is best remembered for his championing conservation, the establishment of national parks, a few spectacular efforts to prevent monopolistic power and his support for legislation such as the Pure Food and Drug Act and the Meat Inspection Act.

However, Theodore Roosevelt desperately craved greatness such as that achieved by Lincoln. That Woodrow Wilson was President when a worldwide crisis erupted in 1914 galled Roosevelt no end and he never forgave Wilson for this. Most biographies of Theodore Roosevelt concentrate on his life before his presidency because this period of his life is far more interesting than the presidency itself. He parlayed his Spanish War experiences into the Governorship of New York. Then in 1899, President McKinley's Vice-President, Garret Hobart died, leaving a vacancy on the

Republican ticket for the 1900 election. Republican Party leaders selected Roosevelt to fill that void.

On September 14, 1901, only six months into his second term, President McKinley died days after an anarchist shot him in the abdomen in Buffalo, New York. Roosevelt, only 42, became the youngest U.S. President to the current date.

The early years of the Roosevelt presidency were marked by vocal opposition to his prosecution of the war against the Philippine nationalists. However, that ceased to be an issue once the American army triumphed under the command of General Arthur MacArthur, Douglas' father. In 1907 Roosevelt sent a Naval Task Force, the "Great White Fleet," around the world to demonstrate to other nations that the United States was now a world power to be reckoned with. Teddy had always been a proponent of American naval power and as a young man had written a history of the War of 1812 which castigated Thomas Jefferson for allowing America's military might to deteriorate.

In March 1909, Theodore Roosevelt left the White House after handpicking Secretary of War William Howard Taft as his successor. The two men had a falling out as Taft was less committed to Roosevelt's conservation policies than Roosevelt thought he should be. Moreover, after four years out of office, Teddy had a thirst for power once again. Roosevelt challenged Taft for the Republican presidential nomination in 1912 and lost. He then ran for President as a third party candidate on the Progressive or "Bull Moose" ticket.

Wounded by a would-be assassin shortly before the election, Roosevelt finished second in the popular and electoral balloting but managed to enable the election of the Democratic candidate, Woodrow Wilson. Wilson received only 40% of the popular vote and almost certainly would have lost if the Republican Party had not split.

Teddy chaffed and fumed through the entire Wilson presidency. He accused the President of cowardice for his unwillingness to go to war when the Germans sank the Lusitania in 1915. He championed the "Preparedness Movement" in which upper class young men trained for war at Plattsburg, New York in 1916. When the United States finally went to war in April 1917, Roosevelt buried his pride and asked Wilson to let him raise a division of volunteers under his command, a much bigger version of the "Rough Riders."

While Wilson may have rejected Teddy's offer on the basis of sound policy, he also did not want TR to be credited with winning the war. All four of Teddy's sons served in the war and his youngest, Quentin, died in aerial combat. Although Theodore Roosevelt is depicted as possibly our most physically robust president, he died in January 1919, an old man at the age of 60. Had he lived, Teddy most certainly would have been the Republican candidate for president in 1920 and would have been elected. TR, not his distant cousin Franklin, would have been our first three-term president.

PART II: The 20th century

For all practical purposes, the 20th century started with the outbreak of World War I. This conflict completely changed international relations for the rest of the century and beyond. World War II was essentially a continuation of the First. Moreover, the Cold War Era, which ended in 1991, was a consequence of the First World War. Without the war and the collapse of the 300 year-old Romanov dynasty in Russia, the Communists would probably not have come to power anywhere.

Not only the government of Russia, but that of three of the other major world powers, Germany, Austria-Hungry and the Ottoman Empire changed dramatically. Indeed, the latter two states ceased to exist. The demise of Austria-Hungry created instability in Europe; the decline of the Ottomans created instability in the Arab world that plagues international relations to the present day.

World War comes to America

Americans were generally oblivious to the events in Europe that contributed to the outbreak of the First World War. Amongst these was the German decision to challenge British domination of the seas by building large battleships, called Dreadnoughts, and the entangling alliances between the various European nations.

Due in part to our common language and heritage, Americans generally were sympathetic with Britain and her allies from the start of the war. Soon German atrocities in Belgium, real and exaggerated by British propaganda, created further moral support for the Allies. With the sinking of the luxury liner Lusitania in May 1915, with the loss of 128 American lives, virtually all Americans, except committed pacifists and those of German ancestry favored the Allies.

There were exceptions, however. President Woodrow Wilson's first Secretary of State was three-time presidential candidate William Jennings Bryan. Bryan resigned in 1915 over what he considered the President's one-sided note to the Germans after the sinking of the Lusitania. He argued that America had never been neutral in that it honored the British naval blockade of Germany. This Bryan contended, was every bit a violation of international law as Germany's resort to submarine warfare. The only reason American lives were not lost due to the British blockade, argued Bryan, was that we acquiesced in it. He contended that Germany was no more guilty of violating American rights than Great Britain.

After war was declared in 1917, the most vocal opponents of American participation in the war were Senators Robert M. LaFollette, Sr. of Wisconsin and George M. Norris of Nebraska. LaFollette was nearly expelled from the Senate as a result. Because the reasons for our participation in the war were so debatable, the Wilson Administration suppressed all public discussion of it. There has never in American history been such widespread suppression of civil liberty and dissent as during World War I and immediately afterwards.

The Communist (Bolshevik) seizure of power in Russia and the several unsuccessful Communist uprisings in Europe produced a "Red Scare" in the United States. Wilson's Attorney General, A. Mitchell Palmer, went on the offensive against any suspected radical, took many into custody and deported them without any due process of law.

The Wilson Administration tried to gain public support by suppressing radicals and establishing a new world order by joining the new League of Nations. Stubbornness on Wilson's part and a politically motivated resistance led by one of the late Theodore Roosevelt's closest friends, Senator Henry Cabot Lodge, doomed America's entry into the League. However, it is very unlikely that the League, even with the United

States as a member would have stood up to Hitler's efforts to reverse the verdict of World War I any earlier than did England and France.

The European War and America's gradual involvement

The causes of the First World War are difficult to articulate. The immediate cause was the reaction of Austria-Hungry to the assassination of the heir to its throne, Arch-Duke Franz Ferdinand, by Serbian nationalists in Sarajevo on June 28, 1914. However, the assassination was a match thrown onto very combustible material.

The Austrian government made demands on the Serbian government. The Serbs agreed to most of these demands. However, when the Serbs balked at letting the Austrians investigate the assassination on Serbian soil, Austria threatened to invade Serbia. This brought Czarist Russia, which considered itself the protector of the Orthodox Christian Serbs against the Catholic Austrians, into the picture.

Russia threatened war with Austria if Austria attacked Serbia. Imperial Germany, which had an alliance with Austria, threatened war with Russia. France, which had a mutual defense pact with Russia, was pledged to go to war with Germany if Germany went to war with Russia. England had secret security arrangements with France.

Germany, during and after the war, insisted that it was fighting a defensive war. It is worth noting, however, that every nation that has started a war claimed to be merely defending itself.

Faced with a general mobilization by Russia, the Germans put into effect the strategic plan it had devised years earlier for a two-front war. The "von Schlieffen plan" called for Germany to throw virtually its entire military might against France to achieve a quick victory and then deal with Russia. The plan also necessitated passage through Belgium, whose neutrality had been guaranteed by the European powers in the 19th century.

At the beginning of August 1914 the Germans launched their invasion through Belgium. This led the British cabinet to declare war on Germany. While the British cited the German violation of Belgium neutrality as the reason for their decision, many British leaders were committed to aiding France in the event of any war with Germany.

The von Schlieffen plan came within a hair of success and as Professor James Stokesbury noted in his *Short History of World War I*, the world might have been better off if the Germans had taken Paris in 1914. If so, the world would never have heard of Adolph Hitler, then a lowly ranked enlisted man in a Bavarian regiment, or Joseph Stalin, a not particularly significant member of the then rather insignificant Russian Bolshevik party.

Meanwhile in late August 1914, the Germans, despite concentrating on the defeat of France, administered a crushing defeat to the Russians at Tannenberg in East Prussia. This elevated two German generals, Paul von Hindenberg and his chief of staff, Erich Ludendorff, to heroic status in Germany. When the war began to go sour for Germany, Ludendorff became the defacto dictator of Germany. Kaiser Wilhelm II and his ministers governed the country in name only. Likewise, Hindenberg was Ludendorff's commanding officer in name only. After the war Ludendorff became one of the earliest prominent supporters of Hitler. Ludendorff's misjudgments and penchant for blaming others for them would lead Germany and the world to disaster twice.

After the German offensive stalled in front of Paris, the war in the West settled into a stalemate. For the next four years, the Germans faced the French and British in lines of trenches stretching for hundreds of miles. Periodically, one side or another would launch an offensive that would cost thousands and thousands of lives to no effect. The Germans were more successful in the East where hardship and defeat had led to widespread dissatisfaction with the Czarist regime.

As the stalemate continued, the Germans considered resorting to other means of winning the war. At the outset of the war, the British had imposed a naval blockade of German ports. Germany responded by resorting to submarine warfare and tried to starve England into submission. However, the use of submarine warfare against civilian ships created a danger of bringing the United States into the war on the side of the Allies.

Until 1917 Germany wanted to avoid this at all costs. On the other hand, getting the U.S. into the war was viewed in England as the most likely way to turn the tide of the war in favor of the Allies. The German Ambassador to the United States between 1914 and 1917, Count Johann von Bernstorff, wrote in his memoirs, "England proved victorious because the

German Government did not realize that the war would be won in Washington, while England was never in any doubt on this point and acted accordingly."

In May 1915 a German submarine sank the luxury liner *Lusitania* off the coast of Ireland. 1,028 passengers died, including 128 Americans. Some in the U.S., most notably former President Theodore Roosevelt, wanted the United States to declare war on Germany immediately and bitterly castigated President Woodrow Wilson for backing away from a fight. At this point, the Germans reconsidered the utility of submarine warfare against the civilian ships although they sent a strongly worded note to the United States. The "Sussex note" stated that the United States could hardly expect Germany to allow the U.S. to honor the English blockade of Germany, while continuing to supply Great Britain with the imports that allowed England to continue the war.

In January 1917, Generals Hindenberg, Ludendorff and German naval commanders met with Kaiser Wilhelm II and his civilian ministers. They insisted that Germany resume unrestricted submarine warfare. They assured the Kaiser that England would be starved into submission before the United States could effectively impact the outcome of the war. The renewed German submarine offensive nearly succeeded. However, introduction of the convoy system for merchant ships crossing the Atlantic in May 1917 reduced the Allies losses to a manageable level.

In response to the German announcement that all neutral ships sailing to England would do so at their own risk, the United States declared war on Germany on April 1, 1917. This decision was not universally popular. In the U.S. Senate, 6 Senators voted against the war resolution and 50 members of the House of Representatives voted against it. Opponents of the war argued, as had William Jennings Bryan, that the United States had never been truly neutral in that America had allowed the British to blockade German ports while continuing to supply England. Curiously, the United States did not declare war against Germany's ally, Austria-Hungry, until December 1917 and never declared war on another German ally, the Ottoman Empire (Turkey).

The Germans had one other trick up their sleeve. In March 1917, the Czar of Russia abdicated, presenting Ludendorff and Hindenberg a golden opportunity to knock Russia out of the war at the same time they were starving Britain with their submarines. The Germans facilitated the journey of Vladimir Lenin, the leader of the Bolshevik (Communist) party of Russia, from Switzerland to St. Petersburg (aka Petrograd and during the Soviet era, Leningrad). Arriving in April 1917, Lenin immediately went to work at overthrowing the Provisional Government. What separated the Bolsheviks from the other political parties was their promise to end Russia's participation in the war at all costs.

The Allies tried desperately to keep Russia in the war on their side. The Russian provisional government, led in late 1917 by Alexander Kerensky, strongly opposed any capitulation to Germany. Lenin and the Bolsheviks seized upon the discontent in the Army, where there were widespread desertions and mutinies, as well in the civil population. The Bolsheviks staged a coup d'etat on November 7, 1917 and seized power. Afterwards, a bloody civil war raged for three years between the Bolsheviks (the Reds) and their opponents (the Whites). Despite assistance with men and material to the Whites from the British and United States, the Communist regime emerged victorious.

Ironically, one could argue that the Germans, by resorting to unrestricted submarine warfare in the Atlantic clutched defeat from the jaws of victory. Without the infusion of hundreds of thousands of American troops in France in late 1917 and 1918, the Allies could not have won the war. Moreover, with the troops it was able to shift to France from Russia, the Germans may well, without the Americans facing them, have forced a peace settlement on terms favorable to them.

The new Communist government signed a peace treaty with Germany at Brest-Litovsk in May 1918. The agreement was essentially a complete capitulation to the draconian terms demanded by the Germans. However, it allowed the Red Army to turn its attention to the Whites, whose armies were never able to unite and co-ordinate its operations.

Meanwhile in France, the stalemate on the western front continued. In October 1917 American troops began to arrive in significant numbers. In the spring of 1918, Generals Hindenberg and Ludendorff decided to launch one more offensive to break the stalemate. With the help of fresh American troops, the French and British were able to withstand the onslaught. Then the Allies went on the offensive against the exhausted German Army. By the fall of 1918, it became clear to the Germans that their lines were collapsing and that they must sue for peace. The Allies demanded the abdication of the Kaiser and the new provisional government signed an armistice ending the war on November 11, 1918.

The aftermath of World War I

Due to the deprivation throughout Europe and emboldened by the success of the Communists in Russia, revolutions began to break out all over the continent. Communists seized control of governments briefly in Hungary and Bavaria and launched an uprising in Berlin, which failed. The Communist revolutions precipitated a right-wing backlash. In Germany, one of the political parties formed in reaction to the uprisings on the left and fear of Communism was the National Socialist German Workers Party, better known as the Nazis.

Another major factor in the formation of extremist right-wing parties was the Treaty of Versailles, essentially dictated to the new German government by the British, French and Americans in 1919. The treaty declared that Germany had been 100% responsible for World War I. It also stripped Germany of much of its eastern territory in recreating an independent Polish nation, deprived Germany of its African colonies and imposed substantial reparations on Germany for the damage done during the war, particularly in France.

While the terms of the Versailles Treaty were deemed draconian by the Germans, they were not too different than the terms imposed by Germany after its victory in 1870 on France, or in 1918 on the Russians. Nevertheless, no German politician of any stripe accepted the terms of the Versailles Treaty as just or legitimate and all German parties to some degree hoped to reverse or nullify its terms over time.

The Germans generally considered U.S. President Woodrow Wilson to be a hypocrite. They recalled that during the war Wilson stated that he had no quarrel with the German people, only with the German government. Now that the Kaiser was no longer in power, Wilson had apparently changed his tune. Nothing in the Versailles Treaty was consistent with Wilson's famous "Fourteen Points" speech during the war, which had promised a magnanimous peace.

Among the many lies that came to be universally believed in Germany was that Wilson had tricked the Germans in agreeing to the Armistice in 1918 with his promises on leniency. This, along with the belief that Germany had not lost the war but had been "stabbed in the back" by domestic traitors (Communists, Socialists and Jews), combined with the economic disaster of the Great Depression to bring the Nazis to power in 1933.

The truth of the matter was that Germany was on the ropes in 1918 and the impact of American entry into the war was just beginning to be felt when the Armistice was signed. The American military commander, General John J. Pershing, had planned an offensive for the spring of 1919 involving several million American soldiers. Had Germany not signed the Armistice in 1918, in 1919 it would have suffered the kind of total defeat it suffered in 1945.

America retreated from its involvement in international affairs after the end of World War I. Wilson was succeeded as President by a complete nonentity, Warren G. Harding. Harding campaigned on a platform promising a "return to normalcy." In the presidential election of 1920 the Harding-Coolidge ticket won a landslide victory against the Democratic ticket of Ohio Governor James Cox and Wilson's Assistant Secretary of the Navy, young Franklin Delano Roosevelt. After Harding's death in office in August 1923, a scandal broke concerning the Teapot Dome oil fields in Wyoming. Administration officials benefited financially by making these oil fields, which were supposed to be reserved for the U.S. Navy, available to private companies. Harding's Secretary of Interior went to prison as a result.

Calvin Coolidge, Harding's Vice-President, was able to avoid any taint from the Teapot Dome Scandal and was easily elected President in 1924. He was succeeded as President by a man, who by experience, was clearly the most qualified individual to hold the office of President in the 20th century, Herbert Hoover. The Great Depression rendered Hoover's presidency a complete failure and caused him to be defeated in 1932 by Franklin D. Roosevelt, by then the Democratic Governor of New York.

Roosevelt was a distant cousin of Theodore Roosevelt. His wife, Eleanor, was Theodore's niece. However, unlike Theodore's family, FDR's branch of the Roosevelt family had been Democrats even prior to the Civil War. The new President not only had to cope with the Depression but throughout his presidency he was faced by a new German Government determined, among other things, to reverse the results of the First World War by trickery and/or by force.

The rise of Adolph Hitler

One fateful evening in 1920 a heretofore unremarkable low-ranked enlisted man in the Bavarian Army named Adolph Hitler attended a meeting of the German Workers Party, in Munich. Hitler had been retained by officers in his unit to spy on various political groups. The Army was very concerned that left-wing political organizations would convert its soldiers to Communism, as had happened in Czarist Russia.

The officers wished to find out which of the many new political organizations they needed to be worry about. Hitler was able to report that this group had a socialist orientation, but was vehemently opposed to the Communist call for international solidarity of the working class. To the contrary, the German Workers Party was intensely nationalist. Hitler joined the party, later renamed the National Socialist German Workers Party, NSDAP by its initials in German and Nazi by virtue of abbreviating the words National Socialist.

At some point, the officers noticed that Hitler had very unique prowess as an orator. In very short order, high ranking military men, businessmen scared to death by Communism, nationalist extremists and anti-Semites found in Hitler the ideal vehicle for weaning the German people from their flirtation with Communism and socialism. Within a few years, the Nazi party became the one of the most prominent right-wing parties in Germany. As inconceivable as it might seem, nobles, generals such as Ludendorff, even intellectuals, now followed this 31-year old man, who heretofore had never demonstrated any particular facility in any endeavor.

Many books have been written about Hitler, some focusing on when and why he became a murderous anti-Semite. However, the world is full of would-be Hitlers and the more interesting question is why so many supposedly respectable people supported him.

While Hitler never explicitly promised to kill every Jew he could get his hands on, he was demonizing them and blaming them for all of Germany's problems from the outset of his political career in the early

1920s. Thus, those who lent their active and passive support to him and deny knowing about the Holocaust miss the point. As soon as he became Chancellor in 1933, Hitler demonstrated that his anti-Semitic ranting was more than just campaign rhetoric. He continued talking about the Jews in the most violent way, humiliating them at every opportunity and sanctioning physical assaults--before the German Army and Navy, businessmen and even many intellectuals married their fate to his.

Prior to the war Hitler had been an unsuccessful and largely friendless artist living in Vienna and Munich. He served four years as a dispatch runner in a Bavarian regiment on the western front and received an Iron Cross for bravery. However, he did nothing in the war that foretold his meteoric rise afterwards.

In 1923, Hitler felt that his movement was sufficiently powerful to overthrow the Bavarian government, march on Berlin and take over Germany. He drew this conclusion from Benito Mussolini's successful march on Rome the year before, after which Mussolini established a Fascist dictatorship in Italy.

However, as Hitler and his followers marched on the Bavarian government in Munich from a Beer Hall, the police opened fire killing several of the Nazis, including one standing next to Hitler. However, Hitler escaped unscathed, was arrested, put on trial and given a very light prison sentence.

During his brief imprisonment, Hitler wrote his memoir, *Mein Kampf*, which clearly set forth his aims in seizing power; reversing the outcome of the First World War and ridding Germany of the Jews. As prosperity began to return to Germany in the late 1920s, the fortunes of the Nazi party declined. In the German parliamentary elections of 1928, the Nazis won little more than 2% of the vote. However, this would change very quickly.

By 1930 the Nazis were getting 30% of the vote. The onset of the Great Depression was one major factor in their dramatic gain in popularity. The other was the campaign waged by the German right-wing parties in concert with the Nazis against the reparations owed to the Allies under the terms of the Treaty of Versailles.

In 1929, the Allies proposed the "Young Plan" intended to reduce the burden on Germany to pay reparations under the Treaty of Versailles. However, the German right-wing parties seized upon the plan to rekindle the virtually universal hostility to any reparations amongst the German population. The leader of the most popular right-wing party, Alfred Hugenberg, decided to join a coalition with the Hitler in opposing the plan. This brought Hitler a degree of respectability that he had not previously enjoyed.

Hitler becomes Chancellor

In 1932 Hitler ran for President of Germany's Weimer Republic. He lost to the incumbent, the 85 year-old World War I hero, Paul von Hindenberg. 53% to 37%. This was to be the last free election in Germany for some time.

Hindenberg was essentially a figurehead and Government policy in the Weimer Republic was determined by the Chancellor, a position similar to the British Prime Minister. As one ministry after another failed, a group, including the very ambitious former Chancellor Franz von Papen and Hindenberg's son, convinced the President to name Hitler Chancellor, which he did on January 30, 1933. The Nazis quickly resorted to violence to crush all domestic opposition and within months had established a dictatorship. Army leaders decided to cast their lot with the Nazis as the means for reversing the outcome of World War I. Upon Hindenberg's death in 1934, Hitler became head of state.

Hitler immediately repudiated the reparations imposed by the Versailles treaty and began to rearm, also in contravention of the terms of the Treaty. It addition to suppressing domestic political opposition, he began to persecute the Jews and opened the first concentration camp at Dachau near Munich.

As Hitler repudiated the Versailles Treaty step by step, France and Britain were slow to react. For one thing, with the passage of time, the ardor of the victors had dissipated, while the ardor of the vanquished had not. This phenomenon is similar to what occurred in the United States after the Civil War, when after the passage of years the victors gave up trying to protect the freed slaves from the former Confederates.

Hitler sensed that Germany's former enemies lacked the will to stop him from reversing the Versailles Treaty. Hitler immediately repudiated the limitations on German rearmament and began to mobilize for war. In 1936, his troops crossed the Rhine River and occupied the part of Germany from which German troops had been barred by the Treaty. In 1938 he engineered the unification of Austria with Germany and then soon afterwards starting pressing his demands for the border regions of Czechoslovakia, an area with many ethnically German residents.

This mountainous area, the Sudetenland, was essential to defense of Czechoslovakia. At first, France and Britain resisted German pressure and Hitler threatened war. In September 1938, the English prime minister, Neville Chamberlain and the French Prime Minister, Edouard Daladier, flew to Munich to meet with Hitler.

With a mixture of threats and promises, Hitler convinced the British and French to transfer the Sudetenland to Germany, thus leaving Czechoslovakia defenseless. Chamberlain returned to London a hero, proclaiming that with the Munich agreement, he had secured "peace in our time." However, within a few months, Hitler broke his promise that the Sudetenland was his "last territorial claim in Europe" and invaded the rest of Czechoslovakia. The defenseless nation surrendered without resistance.

After Hitler swallowed Czechoslovakia, he immediately turned his attention to Poland. Before invading Poland, however, Hitler had to deal with the possibility that such an invasion would necessitate fighting a two front war, one with Britain and France in the West and the other with the Soviet Union in the East.

In complete secrecy, Hitler began negotiations with the Soviets, an arch-enemy he had pledged to destroy from the very start of his career. In August 1939, the Nazis and Soviets signed a non-aggression treaty, which also provided for the two to invade and divide up Poland. Hitler's reasons for seeking the treaty are easy to understand. He wanted to be sure that if France and Britain went to war over his planned invasion of Poland that he would not have to fight Russia at the same time. However, both the Germans and the Soviets understood that their agreement was temporary and that eventually the two nations would go to war. The motivation of the Soviet dictator, Joseph Stalin, in signing the non-aggression pact with Germany was more complex and open to a number of interpretations.

Joseph Stalin

Hitler's chief antagonist was a man with whom he shared a total contempt for human life and the rights of others. Stalin's rise to power was equally improbable. Joseph Stalin was born Joseph Dzugashvili in Gori, then part of the Russian empire in 1879, now part of the independent nation of Georgia. Although Hitler was not a German, at least his first language was German. Stalin's first language was not Russian, but Georgian. Educated in an Orthodox Christian school, Stalin became involved in clandestine revolutionary activities at a very young age.

Unlike Hitler, Stalin was not a spell-binding orator but quickly demonstrated finely tuned organizational skills and some facility as a writer on revolutionary and Marxist subjects. Stalin differed from Hitler in other respects; his personal life was more conventional, at least for a professional revolutionary. Stalin married twice; his first wife died of typhus shortly after his marriage and shortly after giving birth to a son, Yakov, who would perish in a German POW camp in World War II. His second wife, by conventional accounts, is thought to have committed suicide in 1932. She had two children.

While Hitler's public persona was one of constant rage against those he regarded as Germany's enemies, Stalin had a very calm and sober demeanor. This led many people to underestimate him--often at a price of their lives. Another distinction between the two men was Stalin's penchant for turning on and murdering anyone he even slightly suspected of being a threat to him, even many individuals who had been very close collaborators. With the exception of his purge of the Nazis' private army, the brown shirted storm troopers or SA in 1934, Hitler did not conduct recurrent purges within his party.

While Hitler appealed to the basest instincts of his followers: jealousy and racial and religious hatred, Stalin most often appealed to humanistic instincts: such as the brotherhood of man. However, when it came to murdering millions of people imagined to be enemies, the two men were cut from the same cloth.

Stalin's exploits in Georgia and elsewhere in the Caucus region came to the attention of the Bolshevik leader Vladimir Lenin. Lenin brought Stalin into the Political Bureau, which governed the party with firm direction from Lenin. Lenin came to regard Stalin as the party's expert on the ethnic minorities that resided in the Russian empire, such as the Georgians. Stalin also established his revolutionary bona fides by being exiled to Siberia on several occasions for his revolutionary activities. During one of these periods of imprisonment, he shared quarters with another Bolshevik leader, Lev Kamenev, who Stalin had shot in the 1930s.

When the Bolsheviks seized power in 1917, they quickly suppressed all other political parties and had to fight a civil war to retain power. The Communists were able to organize a very effective military arm, the Red Army, led by the brilliant orator and writer, Leon Trotsky. Although a johnny-come lately to Bolshevism, Trotsky clearly became the number 2 man in the party. As such, he soon clashed with Stalin personally and on matters of substance. Trotsky, for example, blamed Stalin for the failure of the Bolsheviks to capture Warsaw in 1920.

Lenin appointed Stalin the General Secretary of the Communist Party. In this position, Stalin was essentially the party's chief personnel officer. He managed this position skillfully by placing persons personally loyal to himself in key positions. Just before his death at the age of 54 in 1924, Lenin began to question the wisdom of giving Stalin so much power. However, when Lenin died, Stalin was able to convince the other members of the Political Bureau that Trotsky was a danger to them all. As a result the Politburo supported Stalin as Lenin's successor.

During the 1920s, Stalin consolidated the power of the Bolsheviks in Russia and his personal power as General Secretary of the party. He embarked on an ambitious program of industrialization, which led him to collectivize Russian agriculture. When the peasantry, particularly in the Ukraine, resisted, the Communists took their produce by force and deprived them of their means of support and the ability to feed themselves. In the late 1920s and early 1930s, millions of Russian and Ukrainian peasants starved to death. By some accounts, it was the lack of concern by the Communist leaders about this mass starvation that led Stalin's second wife, Nadeshda Allilyueva, to shoot herself in 1932.

In 1934, one of Stalin's last remaining potential competitors for party leadership, Sergei Kirov, was assassinated in Leningrad, where he was the Communist party boss. Stalin used the Kirov assassination as an excuse to launch a wide-spread purge of the Communist party, although many suspect that Stalin himself orchestrated Kirov's murder.

These purges occurred in recurrent waves from 1934 until the German invasion in 1941. Thousands upon thousands of Communists and others were shot and millions of Soviet citizens were sent to slave labor camps. Most of the remaining close associates of Lenin confessed to treason in public trials. Many of them were brutally tortured and threatened with having their immediate families killed. Some of the confessions were facially absurd. For example, Communists and army officers who were ethnic Jews confessed to conspiring with the Nazis against the Soviet Union.

The purges had a devastating effect on the Red Army as general after general was purged and either shot or imprisoned. Any officer even slightly suspected of disloyalty to Stalin was purged. He had particular animus towards Marshal Mikhail Tuchachevsky, stemming from disagreements they had in Poland in 1920. Tuchachevsky was one several Soviet field marshals who were executed.

Some purged officers survived imprisonment and a few, most notably, Marshal Konstantin Rossokovsky, played critical roles in winning World War II. During his imprisonment, Rossokovsky's jailers, during torture sessions, had knocked out several of his teeth and broken his ribs.

One person whom Stalin always kept in his sights was Leon Trotsky, living in exile in Mexico. A Soviet agent was able to gain the confidence of one of Trotsky's secretaries and then Trotsky himself. Able to find himself alone with the former Communist leader, the agent murdered Trotsky by hitting him in the forehead with a pickaxe in 1940.

The Nazi-Soviet Pact of 1939

The announcement of the treaty between the Soviet Union and Nazi Germany in August 1939 came as a shock to the western world because it seemed so contrary to the principles of both nations. It caused many Communists in the west to renounce their membership and allegiance to the party.

Some of his detractors contend that Stalin was fooled into trusting Hitler. It is more likely that he thought that Russia would be in a better position to wage war with Germany after it exhausted itself in a long and inconclusive war in the west, much like what happened in the First World War. What Stalin didn't count on was Germany's lighting-fast conquest of France in 1940.

Some historians believe that the Munich agreement between France, Britain and Nazi Germany in 1938 convinced Stalin to seek his own treaty with the Nazis. The theory is that the Munich pact convinced Stalin that he could not trust the west and that Britain and France were waiting for Germany to attack Russia and exhaust its military potential. By signing a treaty with the Nazis, Stalin was essentially beating the French and British to the punch and allowing himself the opportunity to confront Germany under more favorable circumstances.

The Great Economic Depression

In October 1929, the American stock market collapsed. Soon the economies of virtually every nation began to contract causing widespread unemployment. This economic crisis had profound political consequences. It made socialism and Communism far more attractive as solutions to economic and political problems. This in turn provoked a reaction on the right of the political spectrum from those who felt threatened by the increasing popularity of the Communists and socialists.

As we have seen, it was in Germany that effects of the Great Depression were the most dramatic. In 1932, the Nazis characterized the presidential election as a choice between their party and Communism. Ignoring Hitler's opponent, the aging Field Marshal von Hindenberg, the Nazi election slogan was, "Lenin or Hitler."

In the United States, the Great Depression resulted in the first presidential victory for the Democratic Party since 1916. President Herbert Hoover, who won an easy victory in 1928, was defeated in a landslide by the Democratic Governor of New York, Franklin Delano Roosevelt in 1932. Curiously, Roosevelt's campaign did not promise any specific dramatic steps to cure America's economic ills. However, with an unemployment rate of 25%, the American people wanted change and clearly had no faith in Hoover's promises that market forces would end the Depression without action from the Government.

Franklin Roosevelt was a pragmatist rather than an ideologue. He had little understanding of economics, but was willing to try a hodgepodge of measures to combat the Depression. Within the new administration there was a battle for FDR's soul, won by the liberal elements, who convinced him to employ the ideas of the British economist, John Maynard Keynes, which were essentially that to end a depression or recession, a government must spend in order to offset the decline in the demand for goods and services in the private sector.

Roosevelt's economic policies temporarily improved the economic situation in the United States, and he was overwhelmingly re-elected in 1936. However, in the opinion of some, he reversed course too early, reduced government spending too soon and precipitated another depression/recession. Only the military spending necessitated by the outbreak of World War II and the conscription of much of the male labor force brought the United States out of the Depression.

Of course, one of the nations to come out of the Depression earliest was Germany, where Hitler's rearmament and build-up of the armed forces solved the unemployment problem. Another nation, seemingly unaffected by the Depression was the Soviet Union, where massive government projects appeared to solve unemployment. However, in Russia, enslaving millions of the regime's real and suspected political opponents was also a factor in reducing the number of unemployed.

The apparent success of the totalitarian regimes in coping with unemployment led to an increased popularity of both extremes in many democracies. The Communists greatly increased in popularity, although more so in countries like France than in the United States or England, which had and have a more conservative culture.

However, even in England and the United States, the political extremes attracted converts. In the United States, left-wing demagogues such as Louisiana Senator Huey P. Long, gained popularity, as did right-wing demagogues, such as the anti-Semitic Father Charles Coughlin. In England, Sir Oswald Mosley formed the British Union of Fascists, expressing unreserved admiration for Hitler.

On the other side, many intellectuals, as well as working-class Britons, were attracted to Communism. One of these, Kim Philby, became possibly the most effective spy in world history. Rising to chief of British counter-intelligence, Philby worked for the Soviet Union, from the 1930s until 1951, when the British realized that two of his principal subordinates were Soviet agents. The mastermind, however, fled to Russia before he was exposed.

World War II

After Hitler invaded the rest of Czechoslovakia, France and Britain realized what a tremendous mistake they had made in appeasing him at Munich. When he began to threaten Poland thereafter, France and Britain began to prepare for war under much less favorable circumstances than prior to Munich. This, of course, led Hitler to seek the temporary agreement with the Soviet Union.

In September 1939 Hitler launched his blitzkrieg against Poland. The Russians invaded Poland from the East. France and England declared war on Germany. Within weeks the Germans and Russians had obliterated the independent Polish state. For a while, nothing dramatic occurred on the western front. Then in the spring of 1940, the Germans achieved a dramatic breakthrough and the French Army collapsed. Unlike 1914, the French did not put up a last ditch resistance in front of Paris, but instead declared it an open city. By May the Germans were marching in victory down Paris' main boulevard, the Champs-Élysées.

The Nazis also nearly trapped several hundred thousand British soldiers on the French beach at Dunkirk. However, a heroic effort by the British brought most of the troops back to England. France surrendered and a German vassal state was created under the leadership of the French World War I hero, Marshal Henri Petain. A few French soldiers escaped to England, including Brigadier General Charles de Gaulle, who had vehemently opposed the surrender.

At this point England faced Germany alone and many expected a successful German invasion of England to follow. Among those predicting a German victory was the American Ambassador to Great Britain, Joseph P. Kennedy, the father of the future President. However, Britain was saved due to the leadership of newly appointed Prime Minister, Winston Churchill, and the heroic efforts of its fighter pilots, who defeated the Germans over the skies of England at great cost. The maintenance of English air superiority convinced Hitler not to risk an invasion.

Winston Spencer Churchill: the man of the 20th century

Although there were a number of people who were critical in saving western civilization from the Nazis, none were more important than Winston Churchill. Churchill was a direct descendant of one of Britain's great military heroes, John Churchill, the Duke of Marlborough, who fought for James II, William and Mary, and Queen Anne in the late 17th and early 18th centuries. His father, Lord Randolph Churchill, was a leading British politician at the turn of the 20th century. Deemed by his colleagues as unreliable, Lord Randolph died at early age from syphilis.

Winston Churchill graduated from Sandhurst, the British military academy, and served in Afghanistan, India and the Sudan. Churchill went to South Africa during England's war with the ethnic Dutch settlers, the Boers, and was captured and then escaped. This brought Churchill great fame at home and he soon entered politics.

By 1911, Churchill was First Lord of the Admiralty, the British equivalent of Secretary of the Navy. As a member of the cabinet of the Liberal Prime Minister Herbert Asquith, Churchill was instrumental in the British decision to go to war with Germany in 1914. It was naval commitments made to France, rather than the publicly stated excuse, the German invasion of Belgium, that motivated this decision.

Churchill was forced to resign from the Government in 1917 when his plan for knocking the Turks out of the war led to a disastrous defeat at Gallipolis. After serving as an officer for several months on the western front in 1917, Churchill returned to the government where he served in various positions during the 1920s. He was steadfast in his opposition for independence for any of England's colonies, particularly India.

By the 1930s, Churchill was essentially a has-been in British politics. He was widely-regarded to be wrong on most issues and a war-monger. His reputation as the latter came about as the result of the hard-line positions he took with regard to Germany, even before Hitler came to power. Churchill was one of those who refused requests from the German government to soften the terms of the Versailles Treaty.

Almost immediately upon Hitler becoming the German Chancellor in 1933, Churchill began to warn the world about him. He clamored for

England to rearm and prepare for war and to resist Hitler at every turn. However, in the 1930s most citizens in England and the other western nations had their doubts as to the wisdom of going to war in 1914 and saw in Hitler's demands about the Versailles treaty some element of truth and even justice.

When Churchill vehemently condemned the decision of the British government to appease Hitler at Munich, few listened to him. However, with the outbreak of the war, the bulk of the British population, realized that this man, who had been wrong about so much, was right when it really mattered.

Hitler saves England by invading the Soviet Union

As in World War I, Churchill realized that to win this war he needed help from the United States and the Soviet Union. Thus, he did all he could to bring the two nations into the war. The American President, Franklin D. Roosevelt, also wanted the U.S. to fight Germany but was hampered by the fact that public opinion in the United States was overwhelmingly against it.

Although other presidents, notably U.S. Grant, Woodrow Wilson and FDR's distant cousin, Theodore Roosevelt, had considered it, Roosevelt violated long-standing tradition by running for a third presidential term in 1940. He won by a much narrower margin than in 1936.

Roosevelt did what he could to help the British, such as giving them fifty American destroyers and ordering the U.S. Navy to help England protect its merchant ships in the Atlantic. Roosevelt was essentially waging a secret naval war against the Nazis and hoped that the German reaction would, as in World War I, lead to an incident that would inflame and change American public opinion. The Germans, in fact, did sink a few American naval vessels, but nothing occurred sufficiently dramatic to alter the prevailing opinion against intervention.

The invasion of the Soviet Union

On June 22, 1941, the Germans launched an all-out assault on the Soviet Union. Many have offered theories about why Hitler decided on such a course, which on its face seemed unwise since he had not yet defeated England. Equally interesting and surprising is the fact that the invasion caught Joseph Stalin by surprise, resulting in horrendous defeats at the outset of the war.

In attempting to understand the decisions of Hitler and Stalin, it is necessary to speculate as to the mindset of two of the most diabolical men who ever lived. Often the most effective tactic is the one that is the most unexpected. From Hitler's point of view, catching the Russians by surprise greatly enhanced his chances of success.

The fact that it made little sense to invade Russia before defeating England, made it far more likely that the Soviets would be unprepared for such an attack. Hitler knew that Stalin had signed the 1939 treaty on the assumption that it gave him more time to prepare for war.

From Stalin's perspective, it made no sense for Hitler to attack him while fighting England, but it made every bit of sense for the British to try to trick him into starting a war with Germany. For this reason, I believe, Stalin ignored the intelligence he received in June 1941 that the Germans were planning an imminent attack on Russia. He most likely believed this information was planted by British intelligence. Moreover, he particularly mistrusted Churchill, who had tried to strangle the Soviet Union at its birth during the Russian Civil War.

In 1918-19, the British and then the United States sent troops to northern Russia to help the Whites defeats the Communists. At first this effort was directed at keeping Russia in the war against Germany. However, after the Germans surrendered, there was what today we call "mission creep." Churchill and many others viewed the Communists as a threat to western civilization and kept troops in Russia in the hope that it would tip the balance in favor of the anti-Communist White Army.

It is doubtful that Churchill's role in trying to kill the Soviet Union at its birth was ever far from Stalin's mind during World War II. Even after they were at war with the Nazis, Stalin believed that his western allies were dragging their feet with regard to opening a second front in Europe. Their motives, he believed, were to insure that the war was won with Russian lives, not British or American, and to weaken the Soviet Union in the post-war period.

In any event, the German attack on Russia in June was virtually a complete success. By December 1941, the Nazis had reached the outskirts of Moscow, surrounded Leningrad, captured Kiev and had overrun much of the western Soviet Union. Then, the Russians launched counter-attacks and the offensives stalled.

America enters the War

Although public opinion in the United States was overwhelmingly anti-Nazi, aiding Britain was a very contentious issue. Most Americans dearly wanted to avoid war. However, the British got what they needed from an unexpected source: Japan.

The Japanese military dictatorship had been waging aggressive war in the Far East since 1931 when it invaded Chinese Manchuria. In 1937, Japan invaded the rest of China, committing many atrocities, most notably in Nanking.

The United States had for years opposed Japanese expansionism in the Far East. In 1941 it imposed severe economic sanctions on the Japanese, particularly with regard to petroleum. The military dictatorship in Tokyo decided that their goals in China and elsewhere in the Pacific would be helped by destroying the U.S. Navy's Pacific fleet in one bold stroke.

One December 7, 1941, the Japanese launched a surprise attack on the U.S. Navy base at Pearl Harbor, Honolulu, Hawaii. The attack was virtually a complete success, destroying many American battleships and killing over 2,000 American sailors. One exception to the success of the raid was that the American aircraft carriers were out to sea that Sunday morning and thus were not damaged.

American public opinion changed overnight and President Roosevelt received almost unanimous approval when asking Congress to declare war on Japan. That, however, left open the question of whether the United States would enter the war against Germany. Hitler resolved that issue by declaring war on the United States. He was under no obligation to do so since the Japanese had not joined him in waging war against the Russians. England now had the allies it needed to win its war with the Nazis.

Hitler miscalculated in much the same way as the Kaiser's government had miscalculated in 1917. He underestimated how quickly the United States could make its presence felt in the war. The Nazis believed they could defeat the Russians and make England, led by someone other than Churchill, sue for peace, before that happened.

In Washington, President Roosevelt and his chief military advisor, the Chief of Staff of the U.S. Army, George C. Marshall, decided on a "Europe first" strategy. Over the strenuous objection of Douglas MacArthur, the U.S. commander in the Far East, Roosevelt and Marshall decided that defeating Germany took precedence over defeating Japan. Even before American troops made it to Europe, U.S. material assistance to England and Russia played a vital role in preventing a Germany victory.

Nevertheless, the first significant American victories of the war occurred in the naval battle with Japan. At Midway in the summer of 1942, the U.S. Navy's victory turned the tide of the Pacific War. From then on, although the war lasted another three years, Japan was virtually always on the defensive.

1942-1943: The Germans appear to be winning

Despite American naval successes against the Japanese, throughout 1942 and into early 1943 Germany appeared to be winning the European War. The Nazis received a setback when the British under the command of the flamboyant Field Marshal Bernard Law Montgomery defeated them at El Alamein in Tunisia in late 1942. This, at least for time being, eliminated the threat to the Suez Canal. However, the first combat between the U.S. Army and the Germans in North Africa in early 1943 resulted in a humiliating defeat for the Americans.

Where the war appeared to be going particularly badly for the Allies was in Russia. The German Army had encircled Leningrad and was starving the city into submission. A third of the city's 3 million people would die in the 2 1/2 year blockade. Although the Germans failed to capture Moscow, they remained close enough to succeed on another attempt.

The Germans' failure to take Leningrad and Moscow was due in part to their strategic decision to concentrate on conquering all of the Ukraine. They planned to cut the Soviet Union in half on a North to South axis by seizing both banks of the Volga River and capturing the oil producing regions in Georgia and Azerbaijan.

In late 1942, the Germans threw most of the weight of their Army at the city of Stalingrad (now Volgagrad) on the west bank of the Volga. The Red Army held onto the west bank by its fingernails. However, the Soviets had laid a trap for the Nazis.

The Russians planned a massive envelopment of the German 6th Army, focusing on attacking the troops of Germany's Italian, Hungarian and Romanian allies who were guarding the Nazi flank. The plan succeeded and in January 1943, the German 6th Army surrendered. If any single event marked the turning point of World War II, this was it.

Nevertheless, the Russians remained in a precarious position even after Stalingrad. In the summer of 1943, the Germans launched a ferocious attack on a bulge in the Soviet line at Kursk further west. The Russians held and enveloped the attacking forces, achieving a great victory in the largest tank battle in history. At the end of 1943, the Red Army drove the Germans out of Kiev, the third largest city in the Soviet Union, which the Nazis had occupied for two years.

The War in Western Europe: the Road to Victory

Despite all the material support rendered to Russia by the Allies, Stalin was not particularly appreciative of the contribution to the war effort by the United States and Britain. Stalin kept pushing his allies to open another front against the Nazis in Western Europe.

American military planners, particularly the Army Chief of Staff, George C. Marshall, agreed with Stalin. However, Churchill insisted on attacking what he termed the soft underbelly of the Axis. English generals insisted that the U.S. Army was not ready to fight the Germans in Europe, citing the poor performance of the Americans in North Africa.

President Roosevelt gave in to the British instead of invading France as General Marshall wished. The Allies first invaded Sicily and then Italy. The greatest contribution by the Americans and the British to the Russian war effort during this period was the constant bombing of Germany. This required the Germans to devote most of their airpower to protecting their homeland as opposed to providing air support for their troops on the Russian front.

Given the mountainous topography of northern Italy, Churchill's strategy contributed little to the end of the war. The Germans, with relatively little commitment of forces were able to stop the Allied advance. When Churchill persisted in his overall strategy of attacking the Germans on the periphery of Europe, the Americans finally resisted and insisted on a cross-Channel invasion of France.

The invasion was launched on June 6, 1944 under the overall command of the Supreme Allied commander in Europe, the American General Dwight D. Eisenhower. Often overlooked in western accounts of the success and heroism of the invasion is the fact that in June 1944 the Soviets launched massive offensives against the Germans in the East.

The magnitude of these battles dwarfed those in the west. As Rodric Braithwaite observed in his book, *Moscow 1941,* "Two-thirds of the German army were in the East even after D-Day. Indeed, had they not been fighting the Russians, they would have been in France, and there would have been no D-Day."

Although the invasion was successful in establishing a beachhead on the coast of Normandy, for several weeks the Allies were initially unable to break out of it. However, when the breakout occurred, the Allied forces quickly drove the Nazis out of most of France. The most successful commander was General George Patton, the very controversial leader of the U.S. Third Army. Patton is generally regarded as capable in waging tank warfare as anybody on the German side.

In August 1944, the Allies captured Paris. In the East, the Russians were approaching Warsaw, Poland. Many Germans were beginning to realize the war was being lost. In July 1944 a group of plotters, mostly military men who had no problem with him when he was winning, attempted to assassinate Hitler during a briefing. A bomb concealed in a suitcase wounded but did not kill Hitler. Hitler and his loyal followers then proceeded to murder every member of the conspiracy and those non-participants who were aware of the plot.

In December 1944, despite fighting desperate battles with the Soviets for Budapest in Hungary and elsewhere in Eastern Europe, the Germans launched a surprise counter-offensive against the Americans. Virtually trapping large numbers of American soldiers in a salient in their lines, the Germans inflicted over 80,000 casualties and took many prisoners in what is known as the Battle of the Bulge.

The Americans were able to relieve their surrounded troops and regained the offensive. They were assisted in their success by the launching of Soviet offensives in January 1945 which resulted, among other things, in the liberation of Warsaw from the Nazis.

In March 1945 the Americans crossed the Rhine River at Remagen. Soviet and American troops met at Torgau, Germany on April 9, 1945. Soon afterwards, the Russians began their assault on Berlin. On April 12, 1945, Hitler thought he had been saved when President Roosevelt died suddenly of a stroke. However, nothing changed and as Soviet troops closed in on him, Hitler committed suicide.

German resistance in Berlin ceased on May 2, and the Soviets began to advance on Prague, the last Nazi occupied capital to be liberated. On May 9, 1945, the German government, now headed by Admiral Karl Doenitz, surrendered.

During and after World War II, the American generals Dwight Eisenhower, George Patton, Omar Bradley and Douglas MacArthur became household names for over a generation, as famous as Grant, Sherman and Sheridan from the Civil War. Of the British commanders, Field Marshal Montgomery was also well known in the United States in part due to his conflicts with his American counterparts. Less well known in the West were the Soviet commanders, such as Georgi Zhukov, Ivan Konev, Konstantin Rossokovsky and Nikolai Vatutin (killed by Ukrainian nationalists in 1944) who militarily deserve the lion's share of the credit for defeating Hitler.

The War with Japan continues

The War with Japan continued for another four months. Although the Japanese had been on the defensive ever since the American naval victory at Midway in 1942, they defended their island outposts in the Pacific to the last man. The United States waged an island hopping campaign, bypassing a number of Japanese garrisons and leaving them stranded. However, amphibious assaults were launched against a number of Japanese-held outposts, such as Tarawa, Saipan, Iwo Jima and Okinawa, which were overrun at the cost of a great number of American lives.

The American Navy, commanded by Admiral Chester W. Nimitz, played a larger role in the Pacific War than in Europe. However, the Army received more than its share of publicity in part due to its commander, General Douglas MacArthur.

Douglas MacArthur remains one of the most interesting and controversial figures in American history. Son of a senior American general, who himself clashed with civilian authority, Douglas MacArthur challenged the primacy of civilian authority to an extent unparalleled in American history.

MacArthur was 61 years old at the time of the outbreak of World War II. He became a general in World War I, commanding a division in France. MacArthur was the commandant at West Point immediately after the War and then chief of staff of the Army from 1930-1935. After that, he became the commanding general of the Philippine Army. The Philippines were an American protectorate (or commonwealth) from 1898, when the U.S. took it from Spain, until 1944, when it became fully independent.

Other active-duty American officers, such as Dwight Eisenhower, assisted MacArthur in running the Philippine military during the 1930s. With the outbreak of World War II, MacArthur disagreed fundamentally with the military strategy of President Roosevelt and the Army Chief of Staff, General George C. Marshall. MacArthur believed the Pacific, not the European theatre, should be given top priority in allocating American military resources.

As the Japanese overran the Philippines, MacArthur initially pledged to stay with his troops and share their fate. Ultimately, he agreed to be rescued by an American submarine, which spirited the General, his wife and young son to Australia. The rest of the American garrison in the Philippines were taken prisoner, including MacArthur's second-in-command, General Jonathan Wainwright, who emerged from a Japanese prison camp three years later, a human skeleton. Many other American POWs fared every less well, dying on the forced march to a Japanese prison camp from their garrison on Corregidor.

After the bloody battle for Okinawa in spring of 1945, the United States began to prepare for an invasion of the Japanese home islands. However, in 1945 American scientists had successfully tested an atomic bomb. In a decision rarely questioned at the time, but fiercely debated since, President Harry Truman, Roosevelt's successor, authorized dropping the new weapon on Japan.

On August 6, 1945, an American bomber dropped an atomic bomb on the southern Japanese city of Hiroshima, obliterating the entire city. An estimated 180,000 Japanese, mostly civilians, died. Many others were to suffer the effects of radiation poisoning for years. However, the civilian casualties in Hiroshima were far less than the estimated 300,000 Japanese civilians who had died in the conventional bombing of Tokyo.

Receiving no reaction from the Japanese government to the bombing of Hiroshima, the Americans dropped another atomic bomb on the city of Nagasaki, killing another 100,000 or so people. The Japanese government then sued for peace. The Soviet Union, which had not until the August bombings been at war with Japan, then entered the fray in accordance with agreements reached at Yalta and in order to bolster its strategic interests in the Far East. A Soviet officer of Korean nationality, Kim-Il-Sung, participated in the Soviet invasion of his native land, with consequences that threaten world peace to the present day.

On September 2, 1945, the Japanese surrendered to the Allies and World War II ended. The occupation of Japan by American troops was met by virtually no resistance. The Emperor Hirohito remained nominally head of state, but Douglas MacArthur governed the conquered nation for the next five years.

Civilian casualties in World War II

The advent of aerial bombing in World War II added a new dimension to the suffering of civilian populations in the warring countries. The Germans indiscriminately bombed English cities beginning in 1940 killing an estimated 60,000 British civilians. Once the Allies gained air superiority, they returned the favor. Although, the Allied bombing of German and other Axis cities in Europe was aimed primarily at Germany's industrial capacity, hundreds of thousands of German civilians were killed in the attacks.

By the end of World War II, most German cities were heaps of rubble. The most controversial bombing attack was the British bombing of Dresden in February 1945. Critics of the attack claim there were no significant military targets in the city and that the attack qualifies as a war crime. There is also controversy as to how many civilians died in the Dresden raid. Some historians estimate that as many as 150,000 civilians died; others estimate this figure at about 20,000.

Conventional bombing of Japan by the U.S. Army Air Corps killed hundreds of thousands of Japanese civilians. Most structures in Tokyo were still constructed of wood and thus American bombing attacks in 1944-45 ignited much of the city, resulting in over 100,000 deaths.

In World War I, the Germans enslaved civilians to work in Germany and shot civilians to terrorize the civilian population in occupied areas. In World War II, the Nazis did this on a massive scale.

One of the most famous incidents of Nazi terror occurred after Czech commandos from England assassinated Reinhard Heydrich, the Nazi governor of Czechoslovakia in 1942. The Germans murdered every person suspected of being connected to the operation--and their entire families, about 4,000 people. They murdered the entire male population of the Czech village of Lidice and enslaved the women and children, few of whom survived the war.

Major German companies, such as Messerschmidt and the Krupp steel manufacturer, employed large numbers of slave laborers. At some companies, particularly Krupp, they sometimes were literally worked to death. Some German companies also took advantage of the Nazi campaign against the Jews, using Jewish concentration camp inmates in their plants. Most notorious was the German chemical company, I.G. Farben, which built a facility near the Auschwitz death camp in Poland and used concentration camp laborers until the individual workers were worked to death or murdered.

In the Soviet Union, the Germans squandered the hostility of much of the civilian population towards the Communists. Particularly in the Ukraine, where the invaders were initially greeted as liberators, the harsh treatment of the civilian population, dictated by Nazi racial ideology, soon turned it against the Nazis. This helped the Soviets wage widespread partisan warfare behind the German lines throughout the war.

The three million residents of Leningrad also suffered grievously. The Germans and their Finish allies surrounded the city for 2 1/2 years. A third of the population, one million civilians died in the city, most from starvation.

The most dramatic atrocity committed during World War II was the systematic extermination of Europe's Jewish population. Often called "the Holocaust," this is an unprecedented crime in human history. While widespread murder of a particular ethnic group, genocide, has occurred before and since World War II, there has never been such a carefully planned, systematic program of murder carried out against one group of people over such an extended period of time.

The closest parallel is the murder of millions of Armenian civilians by the Ottoman Turks in World War I. As horrible as this was, there remains a dispute as the whether these atrocities constituted a premeditated effort by the Ottoman government to exterminate the Armenian Christians and as to whether this is properly characterized as "genocide."

However, Anti-Semitism was at the core of Nazi ideology and the Nazis began persecuting the Jews as soon as they seized power in 1933. The persecution came and went in waves and resulted in the murder of hundreds of Jews on "Kristallnacht" in November 1938. In 1941, at a conference near Berlin, the Nazi leadership decided to kill every Jew it could get its hands on. In Russia, special teams followed the Army advance, rounded up the Jews in each city or village and shot them all. In Kiev, in 1943, 33,000 Jews were killed in one day. Similarly, mass killings occurred regularly throughout the German occupation in cities and towns all over European Russia.

Three million Jews lived in Poland at the start of World War II. They constituted 10% of the Polish population and 33% of the Jewish population of Europe. The Nazis rounded them up in small areas within each of the Polish cities and then sent them to concentration camps where they were immediately killed in gas chambers if deemed unfit to work. Those who were capable of work were either worked to death, executed at the whim of their guards or gassed when they were deemed no longer useful. Only 30,000 Polish Jews survived the War.

In Czechoslovakia, the Nazis moved all the nation's Jews to the Prague Ghetto and then sent them on to concentration camps, first in Czechoslovakia and them to extermination camps, such as Auschwitz. Several hundred thousand were murdered, the vast majority of the prewar Jewish population.

The extermination of the Jews was a central goal of the Nazis, in some respects more important than any other objective, including winning the War. The murders continued until the German surrender, long after all hope of victory had been lost.

The aftermath of World War II: the end of colonialism

The major colonial powers were so weakened by the war that their hold on their colonies in Asia and Africa was broken, although in some cases not without a fight. Indian nationalists under the leadership of Mohandas Gandhi had been agitating for an end to British colonial rule for years.

Gandhi gained sympathizers throughout the world by employing a strategy of non-violence in confronting the British. The strategy was successful in calling attention to the cause of Indian independence and undermining the case of those in England, including Winston Churchill, who wanted to hold onto India at any cost. The Reverend Martin Luther King, Jr. successfully imitated his strategy in the 1950s and 1960s to end racial segregation in the United States.

One of the principal arguments of Churchill and others opposing Indian independence was that it was only British rule that prevented the Indian Hindus and Indian Muslims from killing each other. As the British prepared to pull out of India in 1947, the political leader of the Indian Muslims, Mohammed Ali Jinnah, insisted that India be partitioned into two countries, a predominately Hindu state, India, and a predominately Muslim state, Pakistan.

As Churchill predicted, the end of British colonial rule was marked by wholesale sectarian violence in which hundreds of thousands of people were killed and many Indian Muslims were forced from their homes and moved to Pakistan, while Indian Hindus were forced from their homes and were transported to India. The two nations then settled into a pattern of hostility, both acquired nuclear weapons and have see-sawed back and forth between improved relations and the brink of war.

The hostility between India and Pakistan was exploited by the Cold War powers, principally the United States, Soviet Union and Communist China. Although Gandhi was the spiritual leader of the Indian independence movement, the political leader by the time of independence in 1948 was Jawaharlal Nehru, a socialist, who leaned towards the Soviets in the Cold War and fancied himself as the leader of the so-called Third World. This caused the United States and eventually Communist China to cozy up to Pakistan.

Possibly the most outrageous consequence of this big power play occurred in 1971. Pakistan originally consisted of two parts divided by India. The eastern part of the country, now the nation of Bangladesh, was ethnically different than the western part. In 1971, the Pakistani Army was conducting a genocidal campaign in what is now Bangladesh. The Indian Army invaded Bangladesh won that country's independence and ended the ethnic killing. During this Indian-Pakistani War, the Nixon Administration supported the Pakistanis.

After World War II most of Africa also won its independence from the European colonial powers. As in Asia, this often led to contests between groups supported by the Cold War powers. In the former Belgian Congo, the new government leaned towards the Soviets, until its leader Patrice Lumumba was murdered and ultimately succeeded by Joseph Mobutu, a dictator who supported the United States.

The aftermath of World War II: The Cold War

After its victories in 1943, the Russian Army kept pushing the Nazis westward. By the end of the War, the Soviet Union's Red Army occupied Poland, Rumania, Bulgaria, Czechoslovakia, Hungary, the eastern portions of Germany and Austria. In several of these countries, the Russians immediately set up Communist governments, often led by local Communists who had spent the war in Russia, backed by the Red Army.

In February 1945, the leaders of the Allied powers met at Yalta in the Soviet Crimea. At this conference the Allies essentially divided up Europe into spheres of influence, with the U.S. and England leaving Eastern Europe in the hands of the Soviets. It became an article of faith to President Roosevelt's American detractors that he sold out the citizens of Eastern Europe at Yalta. They pointed to the fact that one of his chief advisors at Yalta was Alger Hiss, later shown to have at least in some point in his life to have been a Communist.

This ignores the reality that the Red Army had millions of soldiers in the nations of Eastern Europe and that the United States and Great Britain had no means to force Stalin out of these countries involuntarily. On April 12, 1945, President Roosevelt suddenly died and was succeeded by Vice-President Harry S. Truman, a man who on the face of it was completely unsuited and unprepared for the challenges of the post-war world. According to most historians, Truman proved to be a surprisingly able leader.

During the late 1960s, some leftist revisionist historians blamed Truman for the start of the Cold War. Truman met Stalin at Potsdam in Germany in July 1945 and according to the revisionists immediately took an unnecessarily hostile attitude towards the Russians. This overlooks Stalin's track record in duplicity. Many a Russian Communist had cause to regret trusting Joseph Stalin just before they were shot.

Stalin was interested in the security of the Soviet Union and thus wanted pliant client states on his borders. He also wanted to strip Germany and its allies of as much industrial hardware as possible to replace Russia's wartime losses.

Revisionists also overlooked the ideological dimension of the Cold War. The Communist movement was pledged to elimination of the capitalist economic system. In the 1920s, Stalin had differed from his principal opponent, Leon Trotsky, in arguing for the need to build socialism in one country. Trotsky argued that the Soviet Union could survive only by fomenting worldwide Communist revolutions. However, it would have been risky to regard Stalin's position as anything other than a tactical move.

Moreover, the Soviet Union had indeed assisted Communist revolutions in Hungary and Germany after World War I and Communists were active soon after the end of World War II in attempting to overthrow the Governments of Greece and Czechoslovakia. Large Communist movements also threatened to take power legally in France and Italy.

Indeed, it was the fall of the democratic Czech government to Communists in 1947 that solidified the hostility of the United States to the Soviet Union. The U.S. responded by initiating the Marshall Plan, sending vast amounts of economic aid to the non-Communist nations of Europe to assist them in warding off the Communist threat.

In 1948 Stalin blockaded Berlin, which had been divided into four zones by the Allies after the War. Rather than directly respond with military force, the Truman administration supplied Berlin from the air, thereby thwarting the Soviet plan to expel the western powers from the city.

The Communist Victory in China

Meanwhile in China, a civil war was raging between the Communists and the Nationalist government of General Chiang Kai-Shek. After China became a republic in 1911, China deteriorated into a number of fiefdoms controlled by various warlords. Chiang Kai-Shek began an ambitious campaign in the 1920s to unify the country initially in an alliance with the Chinese Communist party. Chiang garnered substantial support from the Soviet Union, which deemed China as being insufficiently developed for a Communist government. Moreover, Stalin was extremely leery of any Communist movement that was not completely beholden to the Soviet Union.

The backbone of the Soviet Communist party was the industrial workers of the big cities. China was even less industrialized than Czarist Russia, which made it inhospitable to Communism according to traditional Marxist doctrine. In 1927, however, co-operation with Chaing Kai-Shek became impossible for the Chinese Communists, when he turned on them, killing thousands of their cadre in the major Chinese cities.

At this point the leadership of the Chinese Communist party was assumed by Mao Zedong, a man every bit as brutal as Joseph Stalin and Hitler. Mao was from the start a bit of Communist heretic. Unlike many Communist leaders, Mao was not a university intellectual who had spent years in Europe or an industrial worker. He believed that the future of the

Chinese Communist party lay with winning support from the peasants in the countryside.

In 1934, the Nationalists had trapped the Communist army in southern China and appeared to be on the verge of exterminating the entire movement. However, the Communists escaped and marched 6,000 miles to north central China and set themselves up in a mountainous redoubt. When the Japanese invaded China proper in 1937, the Communists and Nationalists were again forced to make common cause against the foreign invaders.

During World War II, the Communists won the support of many peasants and their army swelled. The chief American advisor in China, General Joseph Stillwell, became very frustrated with what he considered the hesitancy of the Nationalists to engage the Japanese and with the corruption that permeated the Nationalist government.

After the Japanese surrender, the civil war between the Nationalists and Communists resumed. Between 1946 and 1949, the Communists won victory after victory, and the Nationalist government was forced to flee to the island of Taiwan. On October 1, 1949, Mao announced the establishment of the People's Republic of China.

McCarthyism: the Red Scare in the United States

The fall of China to the Communists had a profound effect on American politics. The Republican Party seized on this to claim that traitors within the Truman administration had been primarily responsible for the Communist victory and that the Democrats had lost China. Republican Senator Joseph McCarthy of Wisconsin began to make a name for himself by claiming that the administration, particularly the U.S. State Department, was rife with Communists.

At about the same time as the Communist victory in China, the Soviet Union announced that it had developed an atomic bomb. Thus, America's nuclear monopoly had come to an end far earlier than expected. It also became clear that some Americans with access to atomic secrets were in fact Communist sympathizers. These two events led to a witch-hunt very similar to that which immediately followed World War I. However, this one lasted far longer and had more far-reaching consequences.

The Un-American Activities Committee of the House of Representatives (HUAC) investigated the Communist sympathies of Americans in various walks of life. One major focus was the motion picture industry where conservative Republicans claimed Communist sympathizers were foisting Communist propaganda on the American public. In fact, there were a substantial number of Americans on the left who had indeed flirted with or expressed sympathy for Communism or the Soviet Union.

In the 1930s it appeared to many that only the Communists were fighting the Nazis and Fascists. This was particularly true during the 1936-1939 civil war in Spain. While the Nazis and their ally, the Fascist dictator Benito Mussolini of Italy, rendered critical assistance to General Francisco Franco's Fascists, the Soviet Union was the only power helping the beleaguered Spanish Republic. During World War II, the Soviet Union also won the admiration of many in the United States since it was bearing the major share of fighting Nazi Germany.

Among the highlights of the McCarthy period was the conviction and execution of a married couple, Julius and Ethel Rosenberg, for treason. This left their two young sons orphaned. Conventional wisdom today, based on documents in the archives of the Soviet Union, is that Julius Rosenberg passed classified atomic secrets to the Russians, but that Ethel Rosenberg was probably executed for crimes she did not commit.

Another facet of the anti-Communist hysteria was the rise to national prominence of Congressman Richard M. Nixon of California. Nixon successfully, and at great political risk, supported the allegations of a former Time magazine editor and ex-American Communist, Whittaker Chambers. Chambers claimed that one of President Roosevelt's principal advisors, Alger Hiss, had been a Communist before World War II.

In a dramatic confrontation before Nixon's committee, Chambers produced documents he testified he had hid in pumpkins at his farm, which seemed to support his allegations of his contacts with Hiss, when Chambers had been a Communist party member in the 1930s.

The Hiss case gave credence to the Republican charges of Communist influence inside the U.S. Government and catapulted Nixon to the U.S. Senate in 1950 and the Vice-Presidency in 1952. Ironically, it would be

Nixon, as President in 1972, who would normalize the United States' relations with Communist China.

The Korean War

At the end of World War II, the United States set up a friendly government on the southern part of the Korean Peninsula and the Russians set up a Communist government in the North. Both the President of South Korea, Syngman Rhee, and the North Korean dictator, Kim-Il-Sung, promised to unify Korea and the two frequently exchanged threats.

American military planners did not consider Korea to be vital to the United States' security and were very concerned that South Korea might start a war with the North. Thus, the U.S. was very reluctant to build up the South Korean Army. In early 1950, Truman's Secretary of State, Dean Acheson, publicly delineated America's vital interests in the Far East and excluded Korea.

At about the same time, Kim-Il-Sung, who had been an officer in the Soviet Army during World War II, was lobbying Stalin for permission to invade South Korea. Although hesitant at first, Stalin gave his approval, most likely on the assumption that the United States would not respond or couldn't do so fast enough to prevent Kim from overrunning the South.

On June 25, 1950, the North Korean Army launched a massive invasion against the South. The Communists quickly captured the South Korean capital of Seoul and continued driving south. The Truman administration hastily decided to send American ground troops to save South Korea. General Douglas MacArthur, now 70, was in charge of the occupation and reconstruction of Japan. He was then given command of not only the American troops but also contingents from other countries that sent soldiers to Korea pursuant to a United Nations resolution.

The decision to go to war in Korea was made without a congressional of declaration of war by Congress. For the first time, with the exception of the American Civil War, the U.S. fought a major prolonged war without such a declaration. Since that time the Constitutional provisions regarding a congressional declaration war have been ignored time and time again and are now a dead letter.

The first American troops sent to Korea were little more than sacrificial lambs. They were unprepared for combat and totally ill-equipped to combat the North Korean tanks. Few of these soldiers survived the first weeks of the war and many of those who did were taken prisoner. American prisoners in the North Korean POW camps were treated very poorly and many died.

After almost pushing the South Koreans and Americans off the Korean Peninsula, the North Korean advance stalled. The United Nations forces were able to establish a small defensive perimeter around the southern port of Pusan. General MacArthur then changed the course of the war with an extremely audacious and risky operation.

In September 1950, over the strenuous objection of Navy and Marine commanders, MacArthur landed American troops behind the North Koreans at the port of Inchon, on the west coast of the Korean peninsula, near the North Korean border. The tides at Inchon made the operation particularly risky, but the operation was a complete success.

Soon the North Koreans were in full retreat and the Allied forces recaptured Seoul. MacArthur then overplayed his hand. Communist China had warned the United States through diplomatic channels that it would not react to South Korean troops invading North Korea, but would intervene in the war if American troops crossed the border. MacArthur dismissed these warnings and believed that if Chinese troops entered the war they would be wiped out by American airpower.

Two columns of UN troops, mostly American, advanced into North Korea, separated by a mountain range. In November Chinese Communist troops attacked them in force. Now the war changed course again. The U.S. Marines were able to heroically hold off the Chinese attacks at the Chosin Reservoir and were evacuated from North Korea by sea. U.S. Army troops on the west side of the mountain range fared less well in their retreat.

The Communist forces now advanced quickly and recaptured Seoul. General Matthew Ridgeway took command of the U.S. troops on the ground and was able to launch a counter-offensive establishing a defensive line north of Seoul. From early 1951 to the armistice in July 1953, the war would be a stalemate.

General MacArthur is relieved for insubordination

Early in 1951, the Truman administration began to pursue a negotiated settlement. Douglas MacArthur did all he could to torpedo the effort and openly advocated expanding the war to confront the Red Chinese. He and his Republican supporters called for the employment of the Nationalist Chinese Army against the People's Republic.

The crowning blow was an exchange of letters MacArthur had with the Republican leader in the House of Representatives, Joseph Martin of Massachusetts. Martin had given a speech castigating the Truman Administration for preventing the Nationalist Chinese from opening a second front in Asia with its 800,000 man army. MacArthur wrote Martin a letter endorsing his views, which Martin read on the floor of the House of Representatives.

Why anyone would think the Nationalists would fare any better against the Chinese Communists in 1951 than they did when they were still on the Chinese mainland defies explanation. In Washington, even among those looking for an opportunity to undermine the Truman Administration, there was little enthusiasm for initiating an all-out land war in Asia. There was no stomach for a war with mainland China amongst America's western european allies. When it became clear that MacArthur would not reconcile himself with the policy of the U.S. Government, Truman fired him.

MacArthur returned home in April 1951 a national hero. Hardly anyone had the courage to criticize him or his views publicly and he prepared to run for President in 1952, against Truman, who at this point, intended to run for re-election. The General's presidential campaign quickly floundered and the Republicans chose a much less flamboyant general, Dwight D. Eisenhower, as its presidential candidate.

Truman today is widely regarded as one of the best American presidents of the twentieth century--even by Republicans, who compare him favorably to more recent Democratic presidents. However, in 1952 Harry Truman was one of the most unpopular U.S. Presidents in history. Early defeats in the presidential primaries convinced the President not to seek re-election (the 22nd Amendment did not apply to him). The Democrats instead chose Illinois governor Adlai Stevenson as their candidate.

Eisenhower defeated Stevenson handily in the general election and the Republicans were back in power for the first time in twenty years.

The Korean War would continue for two years after Truman fired Macarthur with many casualties and little gain by either side. A major sticking point in the peace negotiations was the Communist insistence that all prisoners of war (POWs) taken by the UN be returned. Many of these prisoners did not want repatriation and feared being purged. This was not an unrealistic fear given the Soviet's harsh treatment of many Russian POWs captured by the Nazis in World War II.

In March 1953, Joseph Stalin died suddenly and the Communist negotiation position softened. Also President Eisenhower intimated that he would not allow the stalemate to go on indefinitely and that he might consider using nuclear weapons if it did. In June 1953, an armistice was signed and the uneasy peace that persists to the present day began. During the war more than 50,000 American GIs and over a million Koreans had died.

Unrest in the Soviet Empire

Stalin's death in March 1953 at the age of 73 was a great relief to many of his closest associates. After World War II ended, it did not take long for Stalin to return to purging Communists and persecuting, imprisoning and killing many ordinary Russians.

One particularly remarkable post-war purge involved virtually the entire party leadership in Leningrad. Those killed were the Communist leaders who had most closely shared the privations of the civilian population when the Nazis surrounded the city for 2 1/2 years. Their leader, Andrei Zhdanov, was considered by some to be most likely successor to Stalin. The dictator entrusted Zhdanov with the task of persecuting the cultural elite of Russia. Zhdanov was doing an excellent job of this when suddenly he died during surgery in 1948. Shortly thereafter, Stalin had virtually the rest of the Leningrad Communist leadership shot.

At Stalin's behest, purges also cleaned out much of the Communist leadership in other countries. In Czechoslovakia, for example, many of the party leaders were shot during a purge in 1952.

Just before his death, Stalin initiated another purge, which may have been the beginnings of a Soviet pogrom against the Jews. His government accused a number of prominent physicians, many of whom were Jews, of treason. The doctors who treated Zhdanov were accused of murdering him, despite the fact that he had been an obviously very unhealthy man at the time of his death.

Soon after Stalin's death, a struggle for power ensued within the Politburo of the Party, the committee that ruled Russia to the extent that Stalin consulted with anyone. The first item on the agenda of most of the Politburo members was to get rid of one of their colleagues, the Secret Police Chief Lavrenti Beria, before he got rid of them.

By 1955, Nikita Khrushchev, a party leader from the Ukraine, emerged as the victor in the power struggle. During the war, Khrushchev had been the principal political commissar involved in many of the great Soviet victories such as Stalingrad and Kursk.

In the years immediately following Stalin's death mini-rebellions against Soviet rule broke out in several Eastern European nations, notably East Germany, Poland and Hungry. The Hungarian uprising was the most significant. In 1956 Khrushchev gave a "secret speech," whose secrets remained secrets for a very short time. He denounced Stalin, whose henchman he had been, and accused him of murdering many innocent people, including many party members who had been purged and executed.

There has been much speculation as to why Khrushchev made the speech because it undercut much of the party's claim to infallibility and raised many questions as to whether it was possible for one man to commit so many serious crimes all by himself. One possible explanation concerns the death of Khrushchev's older son, a Soviet pilot, during the war. Stalin intimated that the son had defected to the Nazis and sent his widow to a prison camp. Another possibility is that Khrushchev was overcome with remorse for all the crimes he committed at Stalin's behest.

The speech emboldened some Communists in Eastern Europe to try to ameliorate some of the most oppressive aspects of their rule and the Soviet occupation of their countries. In Hungary in 1956, the party boss, Imre Nagy, instituted reforms and renounced Hungary's participation in the

Soviet-led Warsaw defense pact. Nagy was essentially declaring Hungary to be a neutral in the Cold War.

There was an internal rebellion in Hungary in support of the new regime, with citizens attacking the hated state secret police. The Russian Army then invaded, crushed the rebellion with tanks and executed Nagy. The Russians then installed a more reliable Communist, Janos Kadar, in his place.

The Hungarian revolution was an embarrassment to the Soviets but also to the United States. While it proved that Communism had little popular support in East Europe, it also proved that the United States had no intention of lending support to any East European freedom fighters who actually believed what they heard on the America's Radio Free Europe.

Unrest in Communist China

In 1957, the Chinese Communist leader Mao Zedong invited citizens to criticize the government in what was called his "Let a Hundred Flowers Bloom" campaign. Some speculate that Mao initially was interested in how the Red Chinese system could be improved, but that he was astonished by the amount and vehemence of the criticism leveled at the regime.

He then initiated a wide-spread purge, imprisoning and executing many critics of the government. Thus, it is possible that the "Hundred Flowers" campaign was merely a tactical device to smoke out citizens who threatened the party. Mao also launched "the Great Leap Forward" a hair-brained scheme to accelerate China's industrialization. The scheme failed and was abandoned but not before it resulted in the death from starvation of hundreds of thousands, if not millions, of Chinese.

Mao showed that he would brook no dissent within the Communist leadership. When Politburo member Peng Duhai, a hero of the Chinese Civil War and the Korean War, objected to Mao's policies, Mao stripped him of all government and party positions.

The Cuban Revolution

Until 1960, the Communists had no success in seizing power anywhere in the western hemisphere. Whenever a government appeared to be too friendly to Communism, the United States lent support to right-wing politicians and army officers to nip the problem in the bud. The most prominent example was the CIA-engineered coup that toppled the left-leaning government of Guatemala in 1954 and American support for the military coup in Chile in 1973. The latter led to the brutal dictatorship of General Augusto Pinochet, which lasted until 1990.

Living in Guatemala in 1954 was a leftist Argentine doctor, Ernesto "Che" Guevara, who fled to Mexico, where he was introduced to a Cuban expatriate named Fidel Castro. Guevara joined Castro's small band, which was plotting an almost laughable scheme to invade Cuba and overthrow the regime of the Cuban dictator Fulgencio Batista.

Fidel Castro and his younger brother Raul were living in Mexico after having been released from a Cuban prison by Batista. In 1953, the Castros had organized an assault on a Cuban army barracks in an effort to overthrow the Cuban dictator. The assault failed and many of the rebels were executed. For some reason, Batista did not execute the Castros and eventually released them from prison and allowed them to leave Cuba.

Once in Mexico the Castros began to organize another try at overthrowing Batista. They obtained a small boat and landed in Cuba, with Che Guevara serving as their medical officer. The initial landing and engagement with Batista's troops was every bit as disastrous as the 1953 attack. Many of Castro's men were killed, others were captured, but the Castros and Guevara managed to escape and hide out in the hills of southeast Cuba. There they initiated a revolution that culminated in the seizure of power in January 1959.

Castro was initially portrayed favorably in the United States as a freedom fighter, due to his courting of the American press, particularly Herbert Matthews, a correspondent of the New York Times. When he entered Havana, an enterprising entrepreneur in the U.S. marketed Castro hats with a fake beard, hoping to replicate the commercial success of the Davy Crockett coonskin caps several years earlier.

Reservations about Castro began to arise when he summarily executed a number of Batista officials after a show trial at a Havana sports stadium. Then during 1959 and 1960, he imposed a Communist style economic system and drew closer and closer to the Soviet Union. Finally, he announced that he was a Communist.

The hostility of Castro and other left-wing Cubans had it origins in the Spanish-American War of 1898. The United States invaded Cuba and liberated Cuba from Spain. However, the Americans insisted on a considerable degree of control over Cuba's political and economic affairs. It also established the naval base at Guantanamo Bay, which operates to this day. Many Muslim suspected terrorists have been imprisoned there since 2001.

In 1960 President Eisenhower approved a CIA plan to assist refugees from Cuba in invading the island and overthrowing Castro. When John F. Kennedy became President in January 1961, he also approved the plan. The CIA plan assumed that Castro had little support in Cuba and that the Cubans would rally to the invaders. It was decided not to provide the invasion with air support so as to not to make the operation look like an American invasion, but rather a Cuban uprising.

Castro's army easily defeated the invaders at the Bay of Pigs in April 1961. Subsequently the United States had to buy the freedom of the Cuban refugees taken prisoner by Castro. As Castro increasingly interfered with the political and economic freedom of Cuban citizens, many, including some who had supported him and fought with him against Batista fled to Florida.

The CIA initiated several unsuccessful attempts to assassinate Castro in the early 1960s. In the fall of 1962, Castro convinced the Soviet leader, Nikita Khrushchev, to station nuclear weapons in Cuba to protect him from the Americans. When American military officials learned of this, they immediately started planning to stop it. These plans included attacking Cuba, where Soviet technical and military officials were already stationed. This brought the world as close to World War III as it has ever been.

In the end, Khrushchev blinked when the U.S. Navy confronted Russian ships carrying the nuclear weapons. The Soviet ships turned back. However, the Soviet leader blinked in part because President Kennedy secretly promised to remove American nuclear weapons from Turkey, which borders on the Soviet Union.

Hostility between the United States and the Castro regime continued and despite American efforts to undermine them, the Castros rule Cuba over fifty years after seizing power. Their compatriot, Che Guevara, however, could not rest on his revolutionary laurels. He traveled to Africa where he tried unsuccessfully to foment a Communist revolution and then to Bolivia where he was caught and executed by Bolivian soldiers with the aid of the American CIA in 1967.

Guevara has become somewhat of a counter-culture hero since his death. However, had his efforts at fomenting world-wide revolution been successful, it is likely that many who sport his image on their t-shirts would feel very differently about him. He was a violent puritan, with no regard for the rights of those who disagreed with him.

The Vietnam War

The next major episode of the Cold War was the Vietnam Conflict. Now that the Vietnam War is many years in the past, one could ask whether it is worthy of study at all, since it appears to be largely irrelevant to anything going on in the world to today. Except to the veterans and their families bearing the physical and psychological scars of the war, and the many refugees from Communist Vietnam, the fact that the Communists now rule all of Vietnam has little importance. Indeed, when this generation dies off, it may be as easily forgettable as America's war against the Philippine nationalists at the beginning of the 20th century.

To those Americans born after the 1960s, the decade's major feature was the dramatic change in popular music and fashion. However, to many who lived through it, the decade's major attribute was the Vietnam War. Moreover, there is much of a general nature that can be learned about politics, human nature and the political polarization that currently plagues the United States from the Vietnam era. Most importantly, the Vietnam War is a cautionary tale about how American democracy works in practice.

Today's generation of young Americans cannot assume that all our military conflicts in the future will be fought by the infinitesimal segment of our population which has been bearing the burden of our defense (or adventurism) since the Vietnam War ended. The armed forces are largely unknown territory for most Americans today. With the ever-increasing need to protect our dependence on foreign oil, it would be a mistake to assume that there will never be a time when the U.S. government will feel the need to impress into military service large numbers of Americans who would prefer to skip the military experience.

Thus, it is worth looking at the Vietnam experience so as to be prepared for the seemingly inconsequential decisions by our government that end up have a far-reaching impact on substantial portions of the population. It is also worth examining the inherent corruption that is entailed in asking great sacrifice from some citizens and none from others.

The origins of the Vietnam War

What is now Vietnam came under the control of France over an extended period of time starting in the 17th century. By the mid-19th century, the French for all practical purposes ruled Vietnam. One major result of the French influence was the conversion of millions of Vietnamese, albeit a minority, to Catholicism; another was the conversion of the Vietnamese alphabet to Latin script.

French control and Catholicism deeply divided Vietnamese society. By World War I, many Vietnamese, like other national groups, began agitating for national self-determination. In this effort, they were emboldened by many of the pious, high-sounding proclamations emanating from the American President Woodrow Wilson, particularly his "Fourteen Points."

Among the representatives of the various national groups lobbying the great powers at the Versailles Peace conference in 1919 was a Vietnamese nationalist working in France, later known as Ho Chi Minh. The next year, Ho joined the French Communist Party.

During the 1920s and 1930s, Ho traveled to the Soviet Union and China and was instrumental in founding a Vietnamese Communist Party. In 1940, the Japanese occupied Vietnam and soon afterwards Ho returned to his country determined to free it from Japanese and French control.

In 1945, as World War II was drawing to an end, Ho declared Vietnam's independence. The French had different ideas and a long and bloody war commenced. The Truman Administration, worried about Communist influence around the world, gave the French material assistance.

As the war dragged on, the French commanders decided to draw the Communist Viet Minh into a large conventional battle in which they hoped to destroy the Viet Minh as an effective fighting force. They enticed the Communists to attack a French fortress in northwestern Vietnam named Dien Bien Phu. In 1954, the Viet Minh surrounded the outpost and forced the French to surrender, bringing the French Indo-Chinese War to an end.

In the United States, as the French forces were slowly being strangled by the Communists, some members of the American Joint Chiefs of Staff and Vice-President Richard Nixon advocated using nuclear weapons against the Viet Minh. President Eisenhower rejected this advice.

An international conference was held in Geneva, Switzerland to determine the fate of Vietnam. The conferees decided to temporarily divide Vietnam into two; a Communist North Vietnam and a non-Communist South. The conferees envisioned that nationwide elections would be held in 1956 reuniting the country.

The backbone of the South Vietnamese state was two million Catholics who fled the North upon partition, and settled mostly in the area around Saigon. As the leader of this new nation, the United States discovered a bona fide non-Communist Vietnamese nationalist, Ngo Dinh Diem. Unlike most other civilian and military officials in the Saigon government, Diem had not sided with the French during the battle for the end of colonial rule; he had spent most of the time between 1945 and 1955 in exile.

However, as it turned out, the Catholic Diem was an autocratic leader who aroused little popular support, particularly amongst the 80% of South Vietnam's inhabitants who were Buddhists. The disaffection of South Vietnam's rural population provided a fertile breeding ground for recruits to the Communist guerilla forces, which were determined to unite South Vietnam with the North. President Eisenhower provided Diem with money and a few hundred American military advisors. The North Vietnamese Government in Hanoi trained, bankrolled and sent officers to lead the guerillas, known as the Viet Cong. Beginning in 1960, the Viet Cong became increasingly more aggressive in their attacks on the government.

As John F. Kennedy took office in January 1961, the nation was preoccupied with the struggle for supremacy with what was regarded as the

Communist bloc, led by the Soviet Union and in concert, it was assumed, by Communist China. The nation was still reeling from the establishment by Fidel Castro in Cuba, of the first Communist government in the western hemisphere.

The domestic political considerations behind the War

President Kennedy, although genuinely concerned with Communist expansion, was equally concerned with the potential that more Communist victories would provide to his Republican detractors. He knew that if Vietnam fell to the Communists, the Republicans would accuse him of losing it, as they blamed Truman for losing China and not winning the war in Korea. Given his slim margin of victory in 1960, Kennedy could not afford to give the Republicans additional ammunition with which to campaign if he hoped to be re-elected in 1964. Thus, Kennedy dramatically increased the number of American military advisors to the South Vietnamese Army (ARVN) during his presidency from 3,000 to over 16,000.

Our response to the 1950 invasion of South Korea is fundamental to understanding our response to the prospect of a Communist victory in South Vietnam a decade later. One major difference between the two wars is the degree of support the United States received from other nations in the free world. Britain, France, Canada and Turkey were among the nations contributing to defense of South Korea. None of our European allies provided troops to assist our efforts to save South Vietnam. In fact, in contrast to Korea, most of our allies were indifferent or opposed to American military involvement in Vietnam.

On November 1, 1963, South Vietnamese generals overthrew Diem with the acquiescence of the United States Government, and then murdered him. Three weeks later President Kennedy was assassinated in Dallas, Texas.

America's involvement escalates into major ground combat

Kennedy's successor, Lyndon Johnson, running for President in his own right in 1964, became very concerned that South Vietnam would fall to the Communists during his presidency. He feared that such an eventuality would doom his chances for enacting very ambitious domestic reforms in the

United States. Chief among those was a "war against poverty" and an end to racial segregation. The latter, in addition to being a moral issue, threatened to undermine America's ability to combat Communism in the underdeveloped nations of Africa and Asia.

Lyndon Johnson and his advisors determined in 1964 that without a large infusion of American troops, South Vietnam would fall to the Communists. First the President seized upon an alleged North Vietnamese attack on two American destroyers in August 1964 to obtain from Congress authority to engage the U.S. military in Vietnam as he saw fit. Now it is known that not only did these attacks not occur but that the U.S. Navy was inviting attack by supporting South Vietnamese commando attacks on North Vietnam.

The result, the Gulf of Tonkin Resolution, was passed unanimously in the House of Representatives. Two Democrats had to audacity to vote against it in the Senate--in the face of opinion polls showing that 85 percent of the American public was behind President Johnson.

President Johnson was already planning to commit large numbers of U.S. ground forces to South Vietnam. He and his military advisors determined that by inflicting heavy losses on the Communist forces, the United States would force North Vietnam and the Viet Cong to acquiesce in the survival of a non-Communist South Vietnamese Government.

In February 1965, Johnson seized upon a Communist attack on the U.S. Air Force base at Pleiku as the opportunity to begin sending American ground combat troops to Vietnam. Initially, the Administration said that these troops were being sent only to protect American air and naval installations. However, Johnson and his on-site military commander, General William C. Westmoreland, had planned from the outset to send American troops into the Vietnamese countryside to search for and destroy the Communist forces.

The Vietnam War was overwhelmingly popular for the first three years that American troops were fighting the Communists. The Republican Party was even more hawkish than the Administration. Richard Nixon, for one, made sure that President Johnson appreciated the potential political consequences of a Communist victory in Vietnam.

Nixon, embarking upon his miraculous comeback after losing the presidency in 1960 and the gubernatorial race in California in 1962, visited Saigon for three days in early September 1965. Upon his departure, Nixon held a news conference in which he announced that he opposed any negotiations with the Communists unless the North Vietnamese were willing to withdraw their forces from the South.

The former Vice-President also suggested that the commitment of 125,000 U.S. troops, recently announced by LBJ, would prove to be too little. He opined that, "our commitment will have to be more substantial and larger than we have at present."

Opposition to the war was limited to what was generally regarded as fringe elements on a few very liberal university campuses--primarily on the East and West Coasts. Most college students thought very little about the war and at least passively supported it, largely because due to the student deferments from the military draft, it didn't affect them directly.

The Johnson Administration, with Republicans such as Richard Nixon, at its heels, was telling the American people that the existence of a non-communist South Vietnam was essential to the security of the rest of southeast Asia, which in turn was essential to the security of the United States. This argument is sometimes called "the domino theory."

Although based on not a shred of evidence, the United States Government convinced Americans that a Communist victory in South Vietnam would endanger other countries in the region; Thailand, Burma and even India, Japan and Australia. This contention was predicated in part on the proposition that North Vietnam was a stalking horse for Communist China. In retrospect, it is hard to understand how anyone could believe that whether India, Australia and Japan went communist depended to any degree on whether the Saigon government survived. Harder yet to understand is the proposition that a Communist victory in South Vietnam endangered the government and people of the United States.

Supporters of the Government's Vietnam policy often warned that failure to resist Communist aggression in that country would repeat the mistakes made by the western democracies in appeasing Hitler in the late 1930s. The fallacy of this analogy is that there was no credible evidence that the North Vietnamese were puppets of the Chinese. Such a belief ignored thousands of years of history in which the Vietnamese struggled to maintain their independence from China. Moreover, North Vietnam was a poor country, not a world power like Nazi Germany.

The greatest irony of the theory that we were fighting the Vietnam War to contain Red China is that Richard Nixon, when President, normalized relations with the Communist China while the Vietnam War was still going on. Moreover, in the late 1970s the Vietnamese and Chinese Communists engaged in a border war of their own and clashed militarily over Chinese support for the Communist Khmer Rouge government in Cambodia. All that was ever at stake in the Vietnam War was who would ultimately govern South Vietnam and possibly Cambodia and Laos.

The Vietnam War becomes one of the most divisive issues in American History

The War's popularity waned as more and more American soldiers were sent to Vietnam and large-scale combat operations continued. American combat deaths in Vietnam totaled 5,000 in 1966 and another 9,000 in 1967. Since many of the soldiers in Vietnam were now draftees and casualties were mounting, the anti-war movement grew particularly on the college campuses on the East and West coasts. It became obvious that if the war continued many male college students would be subject to the draft after graduation and might be sent to Vietnam. In October 1967, the anti-war movement staged a massive demonstration at the Pentagon across the Potomac River from Washington.

Nevertheless, what destroyed the enthusiasm of the bulk of the American public for the war was the inconsistency between the optimism expressed by the Johnson administration and military leaders and events on the ground in Vietnam. In this regard the winter-spring of 1968 was a turning point for many Americans with regard to the Vietnam War.

The Communist Tet (the Vietnamese Lunar New Year) offensive, which started on January 31, 1968, demonstrated, if nothing else, that an American victory was not imminent, and that a large commitment of American troops would have to stay in South Vietnam and suffer significant causalities indefinitely to preserve the non-Communist government in Saigon. The Communists attacked virtually every major city and town in the country. While suffering ferocious casualties themselves, the Viet Cong

(VC) and North Vietnamese (NVA) inflicted unprecedented casualties on American and South Vietnamese Army (ARVN) forces.

The number of GIs killed in Vietnam each week jumped from 203 in the week of January 27, to February 3, 1968 to over 500 per week from February 11, through March 2. The Communist forces captured a fortress in Hue, the second largest city in South Vietnam, and held it for several weeks until driven out by the ARVN and U.S. Marines. During their occupation of parts of the city, it is estimated that the Communists executed 3,000 civilians.

The VC also staged a spectacular attack in Saigon, in which a commando squad got inside the United States Embassy compound, where they fought a pitched battle until wiped out. The ferocity of the fighting was also reflected by the Nazi-style murder of over two hundred unarmed Vietnamese civilians at the village of Mylai in March 1968 by an American infantry company, one platoon of which was under the command of Lt. William Calley.

Immediately upon the heels of Tet, the Johnson administration announced a fundamental change in the way the Selective Service System operated. As the war dragged on, and American casualties mounted, the administration became very sensitive to the fact that the war was being fought primarily by young men from the lower echelons of society. There was a growing sense that it was unfair that one could stay in school until the age of 26 and avoid the draft. In February 1968, the administration announced that, with the exception of medical and veterinary students, deferments for graduate students would be abolished.

Upon graduation, most students would thus be reclassified into category 1-A, i.e., immediately subject to induction. Thousands of college students became vulnerable to the draft for the first time. Because they had so little time to adjust to this situation, those men most effected by the change were those of the college class of 1968, which included William Jefferson Clinton at Georgetown and George W. Bush at Yale.

In the fall of 1967, the anti-war Senator from Minnesota, Eugene McCarthy announced that he would challenge President Johnson for the Democratic nomination for the 1968 election. At first, McCarthy's campaign attracted little publicity or support. However, after Tet, support for the McCarthy candidacy swelled. In the New Hampshire Democratic Primary at the end of February, McCarthy received only 300 fewer votes than the President out of 50,000 that were cast.

On March 16, 1968, in the wake of the Tet Offensive and Eugene McCarthy's surprising showing in the New Hampshire primary, Senator Robert Kennedy, the late President's brother, announced that he would seek the Democratic Party nomination for President. With the Kennedy candidacy, President Johnson's renomination no longer was certain. Faced with his rapidly diminishing popularity, the President surprised the American public on March 31, when he announced at the end of a televised address to the nation about Vietnam that he would not seek another term as President. Immediately, a spirited contest for the nomination began between McCarthy, Kennedy and Vice-President Hubert Humphrey.

Both Kennedy and McCarthy opposed continuing the War; however, McCarthy accused Kennedy of opportunism--i.e., not challenging Johnson until it was clear that it would be profitable to do so. Humphrey tried without much success to walk a fine line on the War, afraid to break with Johnson, while trying not to alienate those in his party who wanted the American commitment in Vietnam to end immediately.

On the Republican side, former Vice-President Richard Nixon was busily cashing in on all the favors he had performed for Republican candidates and party officials over the last eight years. It soon became apparent that only Nixon could bridge the gap between the ultra conservatives and the rest of the party. While most of the public's attention was focused on the dramatic battle for the Democratic nomination, Nixon was locking up the nomination on the Republican side.

Only five days after Lyndon Johnson announced his withdrawal from the presidential race, another calamity rocked the American body politic. On April 4, while in Memphis, Tennessee to assist African-American garbage collectors in their strike against the city, the acknowledged leader of the civil rights movement, 39 year-old, Dr. Martin Luther King, Jr., was assassinated. A sniper shot him while he stood with colleagues on the balcony of the motel at which he was staying. Upon learning of King's death, black youths in cities all over the United States rioted. In some cities they looted and burned substantial portions of the inner cities in which they lived.

In white America, even amongst those sympathetic with the message of non-violence espoused by Dr. King, the primary necessity was deemed to be a return to the rule of law and order. The rioters thus played into the hands of the candidates who promised to accomplish that, Richard Nixon and the third-party candidate, the racist governor of Alabama, George Corley Wallace.

The possibility that the 1968 election would become a referendum on the war ended on June 5, when Robert Kennedy was assassinated by a Palestinian, Sirhan Sirhan, after winning the Democratic Party's primary in California. In August, Vice President Humphrey won the Democratic nomination in Chicago, while the city's police battled anti-war demonstrators outside the convention hall.

At the Republican convention the same month, a little excitement was provided by the possibility that the most conservative members of the party, particularly from the South, might abandon Nixon in favor of California Governor Ronald Reagan. Reagan left no doubts where he stood on Vietnam. He told the Republican platform committee that he favored a "stand-firm, fight-to-win position in Vietnam."

Nixon provided a statement to the platform committee, which was a model of ambiguity. He didn't want to alienate the voters who were beginning to tire of the war, but he was more afraid to alienate the right wing of his party. Any showing of a lack of resolve might cause the people who tended to contribute money and work for the ticket to sit on their hands. Nixon attributed his 1962 defeat in the race for governor of California to a lack of enthusiasm for his candidacy on the Republican right. He would make sure that these people worked hard to recapture the White House in 1968.

Nixon's platform statement had something for everyone. He called for a new strategy for permitting a phasing out of American troops and a negotiated settlement. He neither explained what this new strategy might be nor what new terms he might offer the Communists. In fact, for four years he would offer North Vietnam nothing but the opportunity to withdraw their forces from South Vietnam. The former Vice-President did not tell the platform committee or the American people that if, as one would expect, the North Vietnamese did not accept such terms, the war would continue indefinitely.

Further, Nixon told the committee that "the war must be ended...honorably, consistent with the long-term requirements of peace in Asia." He did not explain that a honorable peace was one in which the United States guaranteed the survival of the Saigon government, an objective that could only be achieved by the indefinite presence of large numbers of American soldiers in Vietnam.

Finally, Nixon promised to wage the war with fewer men and at less cost. He did not explain how an honorable peace, i.e., the survival of South Vietnam could be achieved with fewer soldiers than the half million who could not fulfill this objective. Once elected he would convince a large segment of the American population that the South Vietnamese Army, which could not hold its own against the Communists, even with the help of 500,000 American troops, could do so by itself. Indeed, virtually everything that occurred in Vietnam between 1960 and 1975 indicated that this was not so.

Weakened by the dissension in the Democratic Party occasioned by the Vietnam War, Vice-President Humphrey trailed Richard Nixon badly in the opinion polls conducted in September. Wallace and his running mate, former Air Force General Curtis LeMay, drained support from both candidates. While racists from both parties were attracted to Wallace, many extreme hawks were attracted to the third-party ticket by LeMay's suggestion that the United States bomb North Vietnam "back to the Stone Age."

As the campaign progressed, many Democrats with reservations about Hubert Humphrey returned to the fold, but in the end Nixon was elected. Although he received 301 electoral votes, as opposed to 191 for Humphrey and 46 for Wallace, the popular vote was much closer. Only 43.4 percent of the electorate voted for Nixon; 42.7 percent for Humphrey and 13 percent for Wallace.

On January 20, 1969, Richard M. Nixon became President of the United States. Many, if not most, Americans hoped and believed that he would bring the Vietnam War to a quick conclusion, as Eisenhower had done in Korea in 1953. However, the War continued another four years with 20,000 more American, and countless thousands of additional Vietnamese, dead.

As the war dragged on, the Army was forced increasingly to rely on draftees to do the fighting. Up until 1968, many young men with enough intelligence, fortitude and money to do so could avoid the draft by simply staying in school until they were 26. Some draft boards deferred young men in certain professions indefinitely even after 1968. Standards for hardship deferments also varied from draft board to draft board and were also subject to vagaries of influence peddling. Two million four hundred thousand men acquired such deferments during the Vietnam era.

Many young men avoided military service by getting a medical deferment. Many with minor impairments were classified 1-Y and were never drafted.

In October 1970, Selective Service Director Curtis Tarr gave *The New York Times* the following revealing statistics. While 24.2 percent of registrants had failed their physical in 1966, that number had risen to 32.5 percent by the end of June 1970. For July 1970, the failure rate was 40.7 percent. Tarr's statistics also defied the conventional wisdom that Caucasians tend to be healthier than blacks on account of their generally greater affluence. In July 1970, 41.5 percent of white registrants failed their physical, compared with 32.4 percent for blacks.

There were also regional and cultural differences among those avoiding the draft via medical deferment. In 1969, 45.7 percent of those taking their pre-induction physical in Massachusetts failed. In New York, 42.3 percent failed. The comparable figures for South Carolina and Georgia were 17.9 percent and 27 percent respectively.

However, while the easy medical exemption was a very popular means of draft avoidance in some areas, one of the surest ways to make certain you would never go to Vietnam was to join the Reserves or National Guard. Once the draft rules changed in 1968, there was another mad rush into the Reserve and Guard. It was generally understood that due to the outcry when President Kennedy called up the National Guard in 1961, when the Communists erected the Berlin Wall, President Johnson would never do the same thing. In 1966, *Life* magazine described the reserves and guard as "traditional sanctuaries from the draft."

In the Korean War, 700,000 guardsmen and reservists were called to active duty; during the 1961 Berlin crisis: 140,000. By late 1969, there were 750,000 army reserve and national guard troops on the rolls; 37,000 were activated in 1968, in part due to North Korea's capture of the U.S. Navy ship *The Pueblo*. No guardsmen or reservists were activated before or after 1968. Only 15,000 of those activated went to Vietnam.

To obtain a place in the guard or the reserves without connections required some effort. Few blacks found refuge from the draft in these components. A Wayne State University study in 1969, characterized the National Guard as, "a haven for white draft dodgers." The Guard, not surprisingly, vigorously denied this.

Conscientious Objection

One of the least effective ways to avoid military service in Vietnam was to claim that you were a conscientious objector. Selective Service only accorded such status to those able to convince it that they had an objection to all war, not simply this particular conflict. Essentially, you had to convince your draft board that you would not have been willing to take arms up against Hitler or Stalin, as well as the Vietnamese Communists.

Mylai & The Calley Case: How much did Americans care about the plight of the Vietnamese?

To many, if not most Americans, the welfare of the Vietnamese was almost irrelevant to the Vietnam War. At no time was this more evident than in the public reaction to the court martial of Lt. William Calley, a platoon leader in a company from the Americal Division. In March 1968, this company murdered at least 200 unarmed civilians, mostly women and children in the hamlet of Mylai.

On March 29, 1971, a court-martial jury of six military officers, five of whom were combat veterans of Vietnam, convicted Lt. Calley of the premeditated murder of 22 Vietnamese civilians. He was sentenced to life imprisonment at hard labor.

One might expect that the public would welcome a demonstration that the U.S. Army did not condone the massacre, which was unprecedented. To the contrary, the American public reacted to the verdict with an overwhelming outpouring of sympathy for Calley. He was lionized as a hero, often ignoring the fact that he and his men had killed civilians, not combatants. A maudlin recording portraying Calley as a victim and set to the tune of "The Battle Hymn of the Republic" became an instant staple of many popular radio stations across the United States.

President Nixon immediately responded by removing Calley from prison and placing him under house arrest in his quarters. There Calley remained until he was paroled in 1974. Nixon was not the only politician pandering to the pro-Calley mood. Many others, including Georgia Governor Jimmy Carter, did so as well.

The Denouement of the Vietnam War

The level of combat in Vietnam peaked in 1968 and 1969. American troop levels reached over 550,000 with almost 15,000 GIs being killed in action in 1968 and over 9,000 in 1969. Then the pace of combat began to decline as President Nixon embarked upon his policy of Vietnamization. One can argue whether Nixon really expected this policy to save the government of South Vietnam or whether it was really designed simply to prevent its fall before he sought re-election in 1972.

In the spring of 1970, approximately 20,000 American soldiers invaded border areas of Cambodia for the first time during the war to confront Communist troops. South Vietnamese soldiers had preceded the Americans into Cambodia. Two areas of Cambodia bordering on South Vietnam, called "the Fishhook" and the "Parrot's Beak" due to their physical configuration, had been major staging areas and supply depots for Viet Cong and North Vietnamese forces operating in the central and southern areas of South Vietnam.

President Nixon announced the invasion on April 30, 1970. He predicted that the operation would last from between six to eight weeks. The primary objective, he told the American people, was not to kill enemy soldiers but to destroy their supplies and drive them from their Cambodian sanctuaries. Nixon justified the incursion as necessary to protect the lives of American troops in Vietnam and to shorten the war.

Opponents of the War viewed the invasion as a major escalation of the war by the Nixon administration and an indication that the President had no plans to withdraw American forces from South Vietnam in the near future. Anti-War demonstrations erupted all over the United States--particularly on college campuses.

On May 4, 1970, at Kent State University, near Cleveland, Ohio, National Guard soldiers opened fire on demonstrators, killing four. However, Kent State became synonymous with the anti-war demonstrations only after the killings. Tension over the administration's continuation of the war had been building at colleges and universities all over the country throughout the late winter and early spring.

After the Kent State shootings, the nationwide demonstrations increased in their intensity. For example, 2,800 students battled 250 policemen on the Madison campus of the University of Wisconsin. Police used tear gas to disperse demonstrators at the University of Texas in Austin. Student "strikes" also came in vogue. A number of schools, including Boston University, closed for the rest of the school year. At Harvard Law School 700 students voted to strike for remainder of the term.

At the beginning of 1971 after months of relatively little fighting, the South Vietnamese Army with the support of American helicopters invaded Laos, ostensibly to cut the Communist supply lines to the South. Due to the fact that very few American soldiers were involved, there was no uprising on American college campuses as in May 1970.

This invasion was every bit the fiasco that ARVN operations had been back prior to the American build-up. A few days after crossing the Laotian border, South Vietnamese President Nguyen Van Thieu ordered his commanders to pull out of Laos as soon as they sustained 3,000 casualties. In a matter of weeks, the ARVN did so, some in a panic, a few hanging from the skids of American helicopters.

After the Laos invasion, American casualties declined precipitously. "Only" 1,380 Americans were killed in combat in 1971, ten percent of the number who died in 1968. About 150 of these were ground troops and helicopter crewmen killed during the Laos invasion.

In the view of Henry Kissinger, President Nixon's national security advisor and a prime architect of Nixon's Vietnam strategy, "the campaigns of 1970 [Cambodia] and 1971 [Laos] saved us in 1972."[2] He made no claim that these operations materially enhanced South Vietnam's survival beyond the beginning of Nixon's next term. The South Vietnamese Army withstood the 1972 Communists' spring offensive only with the help of U.S. advisors, massive American bombing and helicopter support.

On February 21, 1972, Richard Nixon flew to Beijing to cement America's new policy of normalizing relations with Communist China, thus undercutting one of the primary justifications for the Vietnam War--the need to stop Chinese expansionism. Nevertheless, the war continued for another year.

In October 1972, the United States dropped its insistence that North Vietnam withdraw its forces from the South. The Communists stopped insisting that South Vietnamese President Thieu be removed from power and agreed to return the American POWs. To placate Thieu, the U.S. unleashed a massive bombing campaign around Hanoi and the North Vietnamese port of Haiphong for eleven days in December, "the Christmas bombing." Twenty-six American planes, including fifteen B-52s were shot down--with over 60 casualties and 31 new POWs. Approximately 1,600 Vietnamese were killed in these air raids.

Peace talks between the Communists and the U.S. resumed in January 1973. One week after Richard Nixon was inaugurated for his second term, the final cease fire agreements were signed. The last American troops left South Vietnam on March 29, 1973, and the last American prisoners of war were released a few days later. In his memoirs, one of Nixon's two principal aides, John Ehrlichman, recalled the following exchange he had with National Security Advisor Henry Kissinger.

> On January 23, [1973] the President announced the peace in a short, televised address. The next day I talked to Henry Kissinger briefly in the doorway of the Roosevelt Room. After congratulating him, I asked about the future: "How long do you figure the South Vietnamese can survive under this agreement?" I asked him. I expected Henry to give me some assurances. Instead he told me the truth, and it shook me badly.

---

[2] *The White House Years,* at p. 1009.

"I think," Henry said, "that if they're lucky they can hold out for a year and a half."[3]

In December 1974, the North Vietnamese launched a new offensive. The South Vietnamese Army crumbled with a speed that astonished even those who held it in contempt. On April 30, 1975, the Communists entered Saigon and the war was over.

The end of the war, of course, was not the end of the agony for many Vietnamese. Over a million fled from their victorious Communist countrymen. Many left as "boat people" embarking on an incredibly hazardous journey, which in many cases ended in tragedy. An estimated 200,000 Vietnamese citizens were sent to "re-education camps" by the Communists.

There were executions in these camps, although not on the scale of the blood purges that followed the Communist victories in China and Cambodia. For that matter, the retribution that followed the Communist victory in Vietnam did not equal in ferocity that which followed the anti-Communist coup in Indonesia in 1965 after which somewhere between 250,000 and 750,000 Indonesian Communists and suspected Communists were murdered, and as many as 750,000 imprisoned.

The Case That Can Be Made for the Vietnam War

The most legitimate case that can be made in defense of the Vietnam War is that the Communists are, or were, so much worse than our flawed allies, that it was morally, if not strategically, justifiable to prevent them from conquering South Vietnam by force. A decade before in Korea, over 50,000 American young men gave their lives to defend the freedom of the people of South Korea. The South Korean government also tended to be autocratic and flawed. Syngman Rhee, the leader of South Korea during the War had many of the unappealing attributes of Ngo Dinh Diem. Rhee was eventually overthrown by the South Korean military, which for decades maintained a corrupt dictatorship.

However, there can be little argument that the citizens of South Korea are a thousand times better off than they would have been had the United

---

[3] Ehrlichman, *Witness to Power,* p. 316.

States not sent its soldiers to the Peninsula to stop the North Korean invasion. Although one can argue that Korea, given its proximity to Japan, has more strategic value than Vietnam, close analysis would lead to the conclusion that our Navy and Air Force would have prevented a united Communist Korea from threatening Japan anymore than Communist North Korea does today.

Whether the Korean War was worth the effort I think depends on whom you would ask. One could venture to say that virtually every rational South Korean would think so. Somebody in the United States who lost a father, husband, brother or son in Korea, might have a different view.

Normalization of relations with Communist China continues

One of the reasons that the United States and Communist China normalized relations with each other in the 1970s was that both believed it was in their interest in terms of dealing with the Soviet Union. China had developed an increasingly antagonistic relationship with the Soviets, actually engaging in combat with Russian troops at their common border. As far as the United States was concerned, an increase in tension between China and Russia made it less likely that the Soviets would cause trouble elsewhere in the world.

The rise and fall of Richard M. Nixon

If there was one Republican politician who was regarded as the Devil Incarnate to 20th century Democrats, it was Richard M. Nixon. Nixon, a California Congressman, became a national figure when he successfully and at great risk pursued Alger Hiss, a principal advisor to the late President Roosevelt, for having been a Communist Party member in the 1930s. Although Hiss was only convicted of perjury, for all practical purposes, Nixon demonstrated that he at least had been a Communist at one time.

In the context of the Cold War and Red Scare of the late 1940s, Nixon became a hero to the Republican right and those Republicans who viewed the internal Communist threat as a useful political issue. Actually, Nixon had availed himself of Communism as an issue before the Hiss case. He won his congressional seat in 1946 by painting his incumbent Democratic opponent as being blind, if not sympathetic, to domestic Communists.

Nixon used the same tactic in his successful Senatorial campaign in 1950 against Helen Douglas. In 1952 right-wing Republicans begrudgingly accepted General Dwight Eisenhower as the Republican candidate for President, instead of their favorite, Ohio Senator Robert Taft. To placate the right, Eisenhower's advisors put Nixon on the ticket as the Vice-Presidential candidate. While Eisenhower generally kept to the high road during the campaign, Nixon played to the fears of the international and domestic Communist threat. He at least intimated what Joseph McCarthy was saying explicitly, that the Communists had overrun China due to the efforts of Communist sympathizers in the U.S. State Department and that the Truman Administration was responsible both for the outbreak of the Korean War and the continued stalemate on the battlefront.

In 1953, at the age of 40, Nixon became Vice-President and immediately became the most likely successor to Eisenhower. Eisenhower had a heart attack in 1955, thus casting doubt on whether he would run for re-election or live through a second term. At the urging of advisors who wanted to dump Nixon from the ticket in 1956, Eisenhower encouraged Nixon to take the job of Secretary of Defense in the second administration. Nixon saw through this ploy immediately and refused. Eisenhower backed away from a confrontation with Nixon and the Republican right.

In 1960, Nixon won the Republican nomination for President and narrowly lost the election to John F. Kennedy. In 1962, he ran for Governor of California and lost. He bitterly attacked the press afterwards and the conventional wisdom was that his political career was finished. However, Nixon recovered and began working assiduously to run for President again in 1968. He appeared at every Republican function possible, no matter how small and endeared himself to the Republican county chairmen and others who would matter at the 1968 convention.

Events of course played into Nixon's hands. Lyndon Johnson, who became President when President Kennedy was assassinated in November 1963, won a landslide victory when he ran for President on his own in 1964 against Arizona Senator Barry Goldwater. Goldwater was the darling of the Republican far right and the drubbing he took at the polls convinced even many of those who agreed with him that the country was not quite ready for pure right-wing conservatism.

The Civil Rights Movement and the transformation of the Democratic and Republican parties

As President, Nixon embarked on a "southern strategy" with regard to race relations. In doing so, he succeeded in transferring the allegiance of the vast majority of southern whites from the Democratic Party to the Republicans. With the exception of a very brief period following the Civil War, the southern United States was virtually identical to the white racist regime (apartheid) in South Africa. While racial discrimination also existed in the North, Blacks in the South were strongly impeded from voting, attended inferior and segregated schools and were barred to the extent possible from any social interaction with Whites.

In many southern cities Blacks were allowed to sit only in the back of public buses no matter how empty the front. They were barred from public swimming pools used by whites and were not allowed to eat at many restaurants or stay in many hotels. In sum, in the American South, Blacks were constantly reminded that they were considered lesser human beings than whites.

In the North there had always been a vocal minority challenging racial segregation. The National Association for the Advancement of Colored People (NAACP) was formed in 1916 primarily by whites, including many aging survivors of the Civil War and Reconstruction Era. The leading black proponent of racial integration was W.E.B. Dubois. Opposing him was the man considered by Whites to be the spokesman for American Blacks, Booker T. Washington. Washington publicly, although not always privately, eschewed integration as a goal for American Blacks and advocated self-improvement in a segregated society.

World War II was largely responsible for a marked shift in American racial relations. Blacks who served in the U.S. military were not content to be treated with less respect than German prisoners of war. The need for wartime labor also opened up opportunities for black Americans that had not existed previously. Finally, it occurred to many that pronouncements of our government condemning the Nazis' racist policies were a bit hypocritical in light of our own treatment of American Blacks.

Judicial rulings in the lower courts after the war chipped away at the legality of racial segregation. Finally, in 1954, the United States Supreme

Court held that school segregation was unconstitutional. Up until World War II, the 1896 decision, *Plessy v. Ferguson,* which held that "separate but equal" facilities for blacks and white did not violate the Constitution, was not controversial. The decision was not even mentioned in some of the most widely-used texts on Constitutional Law. In its 1954 decision in *Brown v. Board of Education,* the Court found that racially segregated schools were inherently unequal. Looking backward, it is impossible for anyone to honestly believe that segregation was anything other than a constant reminder to Blacks that they were considered to be an inferior and despised race.

Officials in the southern states dragged their feet as much as possible in implementing the Supreme Court decision. In 1957, President Eisenhower belatedly ordered federal troops to protect a handful of black students who were integrating the public schools of Little Rock, Arkansas. This became necessary when the Governor of Arkansas, Orville Faubus, openly defied a court order. President Kennedy was forced to take similar action to protect black students integrating the Universities of Mississippi and Alabama in 1962 and 1963.

The most dramatic involvement of Blacks in pushing for racial integration occurred in Montgomery, Alabama in 1955-56. A black woman, Rosa Parks, refused to move to the back of a public bus and was arrested. The 26 year-old pastor of a black church, Martin Luther King, Jr., led a boycott of the Montgomery bus system by Blacks, resulting eventually in the desegregation of the city bus system. King instantly became the defacto leader of the civil rights movement. He then turned his attention to voting and other areas in which Blacks were deprived of their rights. King was a disciple of Mohandas Gandhi's non-violent strategies for confronting authority. His ability to convince civil rights protesters to eschew violence won them a great deal of support among Whites, or at least those who were not virulently racist.

In 1960 King was arrested in a sit-in demonstration in Atlanta. A call to his wife by Democratic Presidential Candidate John F. Kennedy was instrumental in winning the support of many American Blacks to JFK's campaign. This was critical because up until the 1960s, as a vestige of the Civil War, the Democratic Party had been the party of the white southerners. This began to change as blacks moved north and became an important voting block in several northern states. This had led President Truman to integrate the military right after the war.

As a harbinger of things to come, South Carolina Senator Strom Thurmond, a Democrat, bolted from the party and ran against Truman in the 1948 presidential campaign as a states rights/racist candidate. In 1970, attracted by President Nixon's "southern strategy," Thurmond became the first of many southern Democrats to switch their allegiance to the Republicans.

Peaceful Civil Rights demonstrators were violently attacked in places such as Birmingham, Alabama where they were attacked by police dogs and sprayed with high-pressure water hoses. This also helped turn public opinion towards a more favorable view of granting black equal civil rights.

After John F. Kennedy's assassination in November 1963, the new President, Lyndon Johnson, embarked upon an ambitious legislative program to secure civil rights for black citizens nationwide. With an overwhelming Democratic majority in both houses of Congress, Johnson successfully enacted a statute protecting black voting rights and equal access to public accommodations. Johnson seized upon a window of opportunity to fundamentally change the nature of race relations in the United States, but in doing so he drove southern white voters and many white voters in the North into the hands of the Republican Party.

The efforts of President Johnson and Martin Luther King, Jr. were undercut by a series of riots that erupted in major U.S. cities, beginning with the Watts riot in Lost Angeles in 1965. The big city race riots and anti-war demonstrations alienated many white Americans and both Richard Nixon and George Wallace sought to capitalize on this development.

With regard to race relations the Republican and Democratic parties essentially switched sides. The Republicans, as the party of Lincoln, had been home to the few whites that cared about segregation. The Democrats, with the legacy of the Civil War and virulent racist politicians, were indifferent to the plight of blacks until after World War I, when blacks moving north began to form an important block of voters in many big cities.

Lyndon Johnson's voting rights act was in many ways the successor to the Federal Elections Bill, or so-called force bill, introduced in Congress to no avail, by Republican Congressman Henry Cabot Lodge in the 1890s. The Democrats were burdened by the legacy of politicians such as South Carolina's Benjamin Tillman and Governor James K. Vardaman of Mississippi, who were never hesitant to advocate lynching (hanging without a trial) for blacks suspected of violent crime. Hundreds of blacks were lynched across the South, mostly between 1890 and 1914.

One can, and many of his detractors have, questioned Lyndon Johnson's motivation in pushing his civil rights legislation. However, anyone whose deeds appear altruistic at first glance can be accused of a self-serving motive. In contrast, it is harder to speculate that those who opposed civil rights for American blacks had any motive other than that they espoused.

Looking backward, it appears that if LBJ thought winning basic civil war rights was going to be helpful to the Democratic Party, he miscalculated. Certainly, Nixon's victories in both 1968 and 1972 were in large part the result of white backlash to the civil rights movement, the riots and the anti-war movement.

Watergate

Richard Nixon is most famous for being the only U.S. President to resign from office. He did so on August 9, 1974, after having been impeached (indicted) by the House of Representatives and having been advised that he was very likely going to be removed from office by the United States Senate.

This was a dramatic reversal of fortune for a man who won re-election less than two years before in a historic landslide. Nixon defeated his Democratic opponent George McGovern by getting 63% of the popular vote and carrying every state except for Massachusetts. In 1972 Nixon had convinced the American people that he was bringing the Vietnam War to an honorable conclusion and that the Democratic Party had been taken over by dangerous radicals.

In 1970, the Democrats had fared very well in the congressional elections. Some opinion polls indicated that Senator Edmund Muskie, then the likely Democratic candidate in 1972, had an excellent chance of defeating Nixon. The President and his advisors decided to leave nothing to chance and embarked on a multi-faceted campaign of spying and sabotage to undermine the Democratic Party.

One aspect of this campaign was the burglary of the Democratic Party headquarters at the Watergate condominium in Washington in June 1972. A security guard at the Watergate noticed that the door to Democratic Party headquarters had been taped so that it would not lock, so he removed the tape. On subsequent tours through the building the guard noticed that the tape had been replaced so he called the police.

The police found several of the burglars in the Democrats' office and arrested them. The burglars consisted of a group of anti-Castro refugees led by a former CIA operative, James McChord. The burglars were looking for material that would compromise the Democrats, particularly Lawrence O'Brien, the head of the Democratic National Committee. McChord gave an alias to the police. However, they discovered that he was a paid security consultant to Nixon's Committee to Re-elect the President, headed by the Attorney General, John Mitchell.

As criminal proceedings proceeded against the burglars and McChord, Nixon and his advisors sought to cover up involvement of higher-level officials. They hoped to cut the inquiry off at the level of McChord. However, a Federal District Court Judge, John Sirica, refused to accept McChord's guilty plea without further explanation from him regarding the involvement of others.

At about the same time, two reporters from *The Washington Post,* Bob Woodward and Carl Bernstein began to dig deeper into the Watergate story aided by Mark Felt, a disaffected FBI official. The *Post* began to run stories daily about Watergate and both houses of Congress began investigations into the affair.

The 1972 presidential election was unaffected by the Watergate break-in which had occurred several months previously. President Nixon won re-election in a landslide and one week after his second inauguration the United States signed a peace treaty bringing the American part of the Vietnam War to an end.

In 1973 public interest in the Watergate story began to pick up. During the year, Nixon's insurance policy against impeachment evaporated.

His vice-president, Spiro Agnew, was not only detested by Democrats, but was generally considered unfit for the highest office. Nixon could believe that nobody in his right mind would push for his impeachment if the result was an Agnew presidency. However, in the summer of 1973, an investigation revealed that Agnew had taken bribes while Governor of Maryland and he was forced to resign in October 1973. Gerald Ford, an amiable conservative Republican congressman from Michigan replaced him. The problem for Nixon now was that most people, Democrats, as well as Republicans, could tolerate a Ford presidency and indeed many preferred it.

In July 1973, an administration official, Alexander Butterfield, revealed in congressional testimony that all conversations which had taken place in the President's Oval Office had been taped. Judge Sirica ordered that the tapes be turned over to the Special Senate Watergate Committee and its Special Prosecutor, Harvard Law Professor Archibald Cox. Nixon refused to do so and calls for his impeachment began to increase.

Sirica's ruling was ultimately affirmed by the U.S. Supreme Court. The tapes established that Nixon had ordered a cover-up of high-level involvement in the burglary. The House of Representatives impeached (indicted) Nixon. When Senate Republican leaders advised Nixon that he was likely to be removed from office, Nixon resigned on August 9, 1974. Gerald Ford, who had never been elected to anything more than a representative from a congressional district in western Michigan, became President.

After a few years Nixon and his admirers began a concerted and partially successful campaign to rehabilitate his reputation. It is absolutely true that Nixon and his chief foreign policy advisor, Henry Kissinger, had many important achievements that decreased the chances for the United States to become involved in a major war. Chief amongst these were the normalization of relations with Communist China and a non-confrontational relationship with the Soviet Union.

The Watergate tapes reveal that Nixon made numerous anti-Semitic remarks. However, his decision to resupply Israel during the 1973 Yom Kippur War may well have saved the Jewish state from destruction.

Nixon's legacy in Latin America is less praiseworthy. His tacit support of the coup d'etat in Chile led to a brutal 17-year long fascist dictatorship. His administration's support of Pakistan during its genocidal campaign in what is now Bangladesh is also a major blot on Nixon's historical record.

Domestically, Nixon is often favorably compared by Democrats to subsequent Republican presidents, particularly Reagan and George W. Bush. For example, he signed into law the major environmental legislation. His track record regarding the enforcement of the new civil rights laws was better than he wanted the public to realize. However, it must be remembered that Nixon had to deal with a Democratic Congress and Democratic-controlled U.S. Supreme Court throughout his entire administration.

Nixon's record might well have been far less liberal domestically had the Republicans controlled Congress and the Supreme Court as they did during much of the George W. Bush administration. Moreover, had the Democrats not controlled Congress and the Court, the undermining of American democracy, of which Watergate was only a small part, would never have come to light. The damage to our democratic institutions may have been much more serious and long lasting.

Ford, Carter and Reagan

While Watergate did not impact the 1972 election, the Republicans paid dearly for it in the 1974 congressional elections. Upon assuming the presidency Gerald Ford was almost universally popular, largely due to the contrast between his persona and that of Nixon. However, one month after becoming President, Ford pardoned Nixon for all crimes arising out of Watergate. This turned out to be an extremely unpopular decision, particularly since many of Nixon's associates went to prison for Watergate related crimes. Controversy has raged over the years as to whether the pardon was part of the agreement by which Nixon agreed to resign.

Ford's pardon of his predecessor was a significant factor in his defeat in the 1976 election by the heretofore unknown one term Ex-Governor of Georgia, Jimmy Carter. The Carter candidacy fundamentally changed the path to the Presidency. Since 1976, it has been an advantage for a candidate not to be an incumbent office holder so that he or she can devote full time for at least two years to obtaining the nomination of his or her party. Moreover, the importance of early caucuses and primaries in small states, such as Iowa, New Hampshire and South Carolina has aided little known candidates and candidates at the extreme ends of their party.

What is also curious about the Carter candidacy is that after he became president it was difficult to grasp what it was about him that caused so many Democrats to support him. He was not a particularly good speaker and had none of the charisma of a Roosevelt, Kennedy, Reagan or Obama.

As president, Carter was profoundly unlucky. During his tenure, the American economy was plagued by stagflation, i.e., high unemployment and high interest rates. Then during his watch, Muslim religious extremists overthrew the most important American ally in Middle East, the Shah (Emperor) of Iran. In November 1979, supporters of the new government seized the American Embassy in Tehran and held the staff hostage until the day Carter left office on January 20, 1981. A botched attempt to rescue the hostages in April 1980, which resulted in the death of eight American servicemen, also damaged Carter's popularity.

Carter however, had one monumental achievement in foreign policy. He brokered a peace treaty between Egypt and Israel by which Israel returned territory captured in the Six Day War of 1967. The Egyptian President, Anwar Sadat, paid for his statesmanship with his life. He was assassinated in 1981 and was succeeded by Hosani Mubarak, who ruled Egypt from 1981 to 2011.

Ronald Reagan

In the 1985 popular movie *Back to The Future*, the protagonist, played by Michael J. Fox, travels back to 1955. When he gets there the character played by Christopher Lloyd, skeptical of Fox's story, asks Fox who is the President in 1985. When Fox tells Lloyd that it is Ronald Reagan, Lloyd responds with incredulity and sarcasm.

Had anyone suggested in 1955, or anytime prior to the Republican convention of 1964, that Ronald Reagan would become the President of the United States, they would have been laughed at. By the mid-1950s, Ronald Reagan was a has-been as an actor. He had a fairly successful career as a movie actor, usually playing second fiddle to such stars as Errol Flynn. However, by 1955 his career was pretty much finished. He was divorced from the starlet Jane Wyman and had married a much younger minor actress named Nancy Davis.

Reagan had been a Democrat and for a time had been the president of the actors' union, the Screen Actors Guild. It is generally believed that his political beliefs changed in part due to the influence of Nancy Davis' father and his employment by General Electric as a company spokesman.

Reagan's potential as a future political candidate began when he gave a very well-received speech at the Republican national convention in 1964 in support of the conservative Senator from Arizona, Barry Goldwater. In 1966, Reagan was elected Governor of California, defeating Edmund "Pat" Brown, who four years earlier had defeated Richard Nixon.

Reagan's victory was due in part to the public backlash from the inner-city riots, particularly the 1965 riot in the Watts section of Los Angeles and to the student unrest on California university campuses, notably the University of California at Berkley. By 1968, Reagan was the preferred candidate for the presidency of many right-wing politicians and the southerners bitterly opposed to the new civil rights laws. Regarding the Vietnam War, Reagan was far more explicitly hawkish in his views than was Nixon.

To the Nixon camp, it was the possibility that the 1968 convention might be swept off its feet by Reagan that posed the greatest threat to Nixon's presidential hopes. In the end, the party's far right settled for Nixon, with the expectation that after Nixon completed two terms in January 1977, Reagan, who would then be 65, would succeed him. In 1970, Reagan was easily re-elected to a second term as Governor of California.

Nixon's impeachment very nearly ruined Reagan's hopes of being president. In 1976, there was an incumbent Republican President in office, Gerald Ford. Reagan challenged Ford in the Republican primaries and narrowly lost the nomination to Ford at the convention. Thus, Reagan could only look forward to 1980 when he would be a few months shy of 70. Previously, the oldest presidential candidate of a major party had been Eisenhower in 1956. Ike was 66, but was running for re-election, not a first term.

After stumbling a bit at the start of the Republican primary season in 1980, Reagan easily won the nomination. As his running mate, he selected his principal primary opponent, George H.W. Bush. Although many believed that Reagan was too conservative to be elected, inflation, a stagnant economy, the Iranian hostage crisis and the contrast between his affable personality and Carter's dour persona played into his hands. He won 48% of the popular vote, but Carter received only 41%, the rest going to third party candidates. Reagan overwhelming won the majority of votes in the Electoral College.

The Reagan presidency almost ended two months after it began. On March 30, 1981, Reagan was seriously wounded by a mentally disturbed young man named John Hinckley. Hinckley did not have any political motive for shooting Reagan; he shot him to impress an actress. Had Reagan died, it would have been a catastrophe for the American political system. The far right would have believed that it had been cheated out of what was rightfully theirs and that for which a plurality of Americans voted. Moreover, a successful assassination would likely have spawned all sorts of conspiracy theories.

Many expectations of the far right were not realized during the Reagan presidency. He promised on the campaign trail to abolish the Occupational Safety and Health Administration (OSHA) and to reign in the Environmental Protection Agency's (EPA) interference with free enterprise. As President, Reagan never sought the repeal of OSHA and soon after he became President, Reagan and his advisors realized that the public overwhelmingly supported EPA in protecting the environment. Early in his term, Reagan replaced the right-wing zealots at both EPA and OSHA with moderate Republicans who at least gave lip service to protecting the environment and worker safety.

On many other issues dear to his far-right followers, Reagan also did nothing more than pay lip service. Although, they may have expected him to reverse Nixon's opening to Red China and revert to full support of the Nationalist Government on Taiwan, Reagan did not do so. Nor did he do anything about the Treaty with Panama, which restored Panamanian sovereignty over the Panama Canal, an issue on which he bitterly criticized Carter.

Reagan and the Communists

Those who to this day have transformed Reagan into an American deity, do so on several accounts: he unfettered American enterprise from stifling regulation and taxation and he brought down the Soviet Union. While all these points are arguable, they ignore a number of inconvenient facts. It is true that Reagan markedly increased American military spending. He did this while cutting taxes and creating a huge budget deficit, another aspect of his presidency that runs counter to the "spend as you go" doctrines of the Republican Party.

Moreover, the Soviet Union did not fall under Reagan's watch, it unraveled during George H.W. Bush's presidency. Reagan's admirers often recount his challenge in June 1987 to the Soviet leader, Mikhail Gorbachev to tear down the Berlin Wall, but the Wall also came down in October 1989 during Bush's presidency, not Reagan's.

Reagan enthusiasts also minimize the internal causes for the collapse of Communism. In the 1980s, Communist leaders in Russia, China and Vietnam came to realize that Marxist economics was not working and was impoverishing their countries.

The Communists abandon Communism

Deng Xiaoping, a veteran Communist leader purged by Mao Zedong several times during his career, emerged as China's paramount leader from the power struggle that follow Mao's death in 1976. Mao, unlike Stalin, did not necessarily execute high-ranking party leaders who were purged. Although a few were beaten to death in prison, and all who were purged suffered greatly, Mao rehabilitated some like Deng, whenever he felt it served his interests.

By 1985 Deng embarked on a policy of privatizing the Chinese economy, which resulted in tremendous improvements in the standard of living for most Chinese citizens. The Vietnamese Communists soon followed the Chinese example, while the North Koreans stuck to their guns, leaving their population in abject poverty to the present day.

On the other hand, the Chinese Communists have not tolerated any challenge to their political control of their country. Most famously, the

Politburo authorized the Army to open fire on anti-government demonstrators in Tiananmen Square in Beijing in July 1989, killing hundreds, if not thousands, of protesters.

Leonid Brezhnev, the Russian Communist leader, died in 1982 after 18 years in power. He was succeeded by two aged Communists, who died shortly after becoming the party's general secretary. In 1985, Mikhail Gorbachev, became the party's general secretary at the age of 54. Gorbachev, like Deng, realized that Marxist economics was not working and moved quickly to reform the system.

Gorbachev also refused to sanction the use of force to suppress anti-Communist demonstrations in Eastern Europe. This decision contributed greatly to the collapse of all the Communist governments in those nations between 1989 and 1991.

While it is true that the vast increases in American military spending made it difficult for the Soviets to maintain parity with the U.S., the Soviets continued to have a nuclear armed military, capable of defending Russia's vital interests. It is also true that Reagan encouraged Saudi Arabia to increase oil production and thereby decreasing the price of crude oil, the export of which the Soviet economy depended. However, it is quite a stretch to attribute the fall of crude oil prices to Reagan's genius.

However, the depressed price of crude oil not only hurt the Soviets, but later destroyed the Russian experiment in democracy. Crude oil prices recovered just in time for Vladimir Putin to institute despotism light. In any event, Gorbachev was faced with economic disaster when he assumed power. The credit to which Reagan and his Secretary of State George Schultz are fully entitled is realizing that Gorbachev truly wanted to make fundamental changes in the Soviet system. Over the objections of many of his closest advisors, Reagan engaged Gorbachev and by doing so contributed greatly to the end of the Cold War.

Reagan's second term

In retrospect, the highpoint of Reagan's second term was the assistance he and George Schultz lent Gorbachev in destroying Russian Communism. However, at the time, much of the energy of the administration was spent dealing with the Iran Contra affair.

In 1979, a leftist anti-American party, the Sandinistas, took power in Nicaragua. Fearing the spread of Communism in Latin America, Reagan dearly wanted to give all the support possible to the opponents of the new regime, the Contras. However, many Americans feared that the United States could find itself embroiled in a Central American civil war similar to Vietnam. Moreover, many of the Contras had been members of the police and military of Nicaragua's former right-wing dictator, Anastasio Samoza.

The Democratic-controlled Congress passed a resolution barring American aid to the Contras. Afterwards, Reagan was never quite successful in convincing the American people that the Sandinistas posed a threat to American security and the congressional prohibition against aid to the Nicaraguan Contras remained in force.

Meanwhile, the Iranian backed terrorists in Lebanon, Hezbollah, had taken a number of Americans hostage. At the same time, Iran was engaged in its war with Iraq and Saddam Hussein. The Iranians desperately needed spare parts for American equipment they had inherited from the Shah. A number of White House advisors, the most famous of which was Marine Lt. Col. Oliver North, came up a brilliant idea. They proposed providing the Iranians American spare parts through the Israelis and then using the proceeds of these weapons sales to fund the Contras in Nicaragua. This endeavor was in direct contravention of the congressional prohibition and raised serious Constitutional issues.

In the congressional hearings looking into the affair, North emerged as somewhat of a hero to much of the American public. It is most likely that most Americans had no problem with the administration ignoring the Constitution to aid the Contras in their fight with the Sandinistas. However, the effort to pay the Iranians for help in gaining the release of the hostages was not popular.

Reagan denied knowing that the weapons were being given to the Iranians in order to bribe them in assisting in the release of hostages. In retrospect, it may be that he was not lying because it is unclear when he began to develop Alzheimer's disease, which became more evident after he left office.

In any event, Iran-Contra was a fiasco for the Reagan administration and markedly decreased Reagan's popularity towards the end of his term.

This gave the Democrats some hope for winning the 1988 presidential election. This hope was destroyed by the nomination of Massachusetts Governor Michael Dukakis, possibly the most uninspiring presidential candidate ever nominated by a major party.

The Reagan legacy

Remaking the American judicial system

One aspect in which Reagan had a lasting impact was changing the focus of the American judicial system. He appointed very conservative judges to the bench at all levels and transformed the federal courts from a sympathetic orientation towards criminal defendants' rights and government regulation to an orientation sympathetic to business interests and prosecutors and the police. His judicial appointments were hostile to organized labor, a backbone of the political support of the Democratic Party.

Reagan also appointed younger men to the bench so that twenty two years after he left office, judges like Antonin Scalia and Anthony Kennedy, still sit on the U.S. Supreme Court. His Bush successors followed suit with the appointments of Clarence Thomas, John Roberts and Samuel Alito, thus virtually assuring a conservative orientation on the court whether or not the political tide oscillates back towards liberalism.

Reagan also changed the orientation of the Republican Party. Ironically, the fall of the Soviet Union deprived the Republicans one of their major selling points--fear of Communism. Reagan replaced it with an oscillating ideology; anti-tax and anti-debt.

Reagan embraced what was termed "supply-side" economics, which essentially argues that virtually all taxes are bad and that lower and less progressive taxes promote economic growth and prosperity for all. However, since Reagan, whenever the United States accumulates debt, the Republicans switch gears to advocate the need to cut spending on all domestic programs which benefit those at the lower end of the economic spectrum. Curiously most white voters particularly in the poorest states, seem to have embraced this ideology. This phenomenon was examined in detail by Thomas Frank in his book, *What's the Matter with Kansas*.

Back in the 1930s, Louisiana Senator Huey dominated his state politics and prior to his assassination in 1935 threatened to become a legitimate presidential possibility. Unlike many southern politicians, Long rarely, if ever, relied on racial prejudice to win elections. His appeal, "Share the Wealth," was directed at poor white voters. Since Reagan, poor whites, unlike those who supported Huey Long, seem to believe making the rich richer will eventually trickle down to them.

George H.W. Bush

Reagan's far-right supporters were never completely comfortable with George H. W. Bush. Bush moved to Texas after graduating from Yale and made his fortune in the petroleum industry before entering politics. However, the conservative right suspected that he was at heart a Rockefeller Republican. Bush's father had been a U.S. Senator from Connecticut and his family was well-connected to Wall Street. Moreover, many on the right never forgave Bush's criticism of Reagan during the 1980 campaign, particularly, his spot-on characterization of Reagan's supply-side mantra as "voodoo economics."

Whatever good will Bush gained on the right by his nomination of Clarence Thomas to the Supreme Court was cancelled out by his nomination of David Souter, who turned out to be one of the more liberal justices. Bush felt obligated to reduce the substantial debt created by Reagan's prolific military spending and lowering of taxes. However, he needed the co-operation of the Democratic Congress to do so.

In reaching a compromise with the Democrats and attacking the debt by raising taxes and cutting federal spending, Bush reneged on signature campaign promises. He became an anathema to the conservatives, despite the fact that in retrospect, his willingness to attack the debt left by Reagan was instrumental in ushering in the prosperity of the 1990s.

For conservatives, Bush's heresy on taxation negated everything else his did, including his extremely popular stewardship of the 1991 Gulf War. Thus, in the election of 1992, many either stayed home or voted for the third-party candidate Ross Perot. Perot received 19% of the popular vote, the most by any third-party candidate other than ex-President Theodore Roosevelt in 1912. Since Perot's campaign put forth little in the way of concrete ideas for the country's economic problems, much of the Perot vote was cast to punish Bush. By doing so, the conservatives contributed greatly to the election of Bill Clinton.

Bush's historical legacy will ultimately rest on his decision to force Saddam Hussein out of Kuwait and his decision, reversed by his son twelve years later, not to drive Saddam out of power. First of all, the Bush Administration very skillfully organized a coalition which included many Arab countries to undo the Iraqi invasion of Kuwait.

One could argue that the war was unnecessary in that Saddam had a colorable claim on Kuwait, whose separation from Iraq was accomplished by the British colonialists. In Saddam's view, the Europeans had no right to do this. Moreover, he believed he had a legitimate grievance against the Kuwaiti royal family for undercutting his efforts to maintain a relatively high price of crude oil.

On the other hand, Bush had a legitimate concern that to allow Saddam to control oil-rich Kuwait would come back to haunt the West and that it would embolden him to take aggressive action against the near-by Saudi oil fields, so critical to western oil supplies. Harkening back to the historical lessons drawn from World War II, one could argue that Bush in 1991 did to Saddam what the British and French should have done to Hitler in 1936. On the other hand, since World War II this analogy is espoused everytime a leader wants to start a war--most notably to justify sending ground American troops to Vietnam.

With relatively minimal losses, the American-led coalition force destroyed much of the Iraqi army and forced Saddam to abandon Kuwait. However, Bush stopped short of driving on to Baghdad and toppling Saddam from power. The West quickly established a no-fly zone over northern Iraq to protect the Kurdish minority and the oil fields in that region. However, it allowed Saddam to brutally crush a Shiite rebellion, which the western powers had encouraged.

One could not have handled the Iraqi invasion of Kuwait more skillfully. Bush forced Saddam out of Kuwait and crippled his ability to wage further aggression against his neighbors. He left a Sunni and secularist Iraqi dictatorship in power as a powerful counterweight to designs of equally aggressive Shiite Iran.

William Jefferson "Bill" Clinton also had a very peculiar path to the presidency. Before his birth his biological father died in an auto accident. Like Gerald Ford, Clinton acquired the name by which history knows him when his stepfather adopted him.

A precocious child, Clinton was raised in Arkansas by his mother and alcoholic stepfather. Clinton went to Georgetown University and graduated in 1968, at the height of the Vietnam War draft. As did many of his generation, he avoided Vietnam service, however he did so in a more ingenious way than others. His successor, George W. Bush, joined the Texas Air National Guard, which virtually assured that he would never perform military service overseas.

Clinton's draft board dragged its feat in inducting him and even took the unusual step of rescinding his draft notice. This enabled Clinton to go to England to study at Oxford. Later, he committed to attending the University of Arkansas Law School and joining the ROTC (Reserve Officers Training Corps) unit there. This resulted in a change in his classification for the draft and insured that he would not be ordered to report for induction.

After the draft lottery was instituted in December 1969, Clinton received a high enough lottery number than he was no longer in danger of being drafted. He gave up his student deferment and rescinded his commitment to the Arkansas Law School and its ROTC unit. After completing his studies at Oxford, Clinton attended Yale Law School were he met his wife, Hillary Rodham, a fellow Yale Law Student.

Clinton had presidential ambitions from an early age. However, one must marvel the path by which he sought to achieve this goal. After losing a race for a congressional seat from Arkansas, Clinton was elected Attorney General of Arkansas in 1976 and then elected Governor in 1978. In retrospect it seems that it would very unlikely for someone to parley the governorship of a small state like Arkansas into the presidency.

Clinton's ambitions were almost derailed at several junctures. In 1980 he was defeated for re-election. This was due in part to the Reagan landslide, but also to unhappiness among Arkansas residents at the Carter administration's decision to send many criminals released from Cuban jails by Fidel Castro to Arkansas prisons.

In 1982 Clinton won his Governorship back and was re-elected in 1984, 1986 and 1990 (the Governor's term increased from 2 years to 4 years after the 1986 election). In 1988, as a rising star in the Party, Clinton was selected as the keynote speaker at the Democratic National Convention. His speech was a resounding dud, almost assuring his disappearance from the national scene.

Nevertheless, after being re-elected Governor in 1990, Clinton began his campaign for the Democratic nomination. President Bush's extremely high approval ratings following the Gulf War in 1991 scared off many other aspirants and Clinton easily won the Democratic nomination. Then, in part due to the souring economy, conservative disenchantment with Bush and Ross Perot's third-party candidacy, Clinton defeated President Bush in the general election.

The Clinton presidency began, as do all others, with rewards for the groups whose money and grass roots efforts contributed significantly to his election victory. For Clinton, one of those groups was the gay community, who he rewarded with the "don't ask, don't tell" policy which allowed gay citizens to serve in the armed forces so long as they did not publicize their sexual orientation.

Another major initiative of the Clinton administration was its effort to obtain health insurance for all American citizens. Intensive lobbying by the health insurance industry and lock-step opposition from most of the Republican Party doomed Clinton's health care initiative to failure.

Clinton was far more successful in reducing the national debt and pursuing economic policies that made his tenure one of unparalleled prosperity. In the 1994 congressional elections, the Republicans won control of Congress and were determined to reduce the debt and the budget deficit solely by slashing domestic programs. Clinton called their bluff and refused to sign the Republican budget, thus shutting down much of the non-defense functions of the Federal Government for several weeks in late 1995 and January 1996. In the end, the Republicans blinked, agreed to less cuts in domestic spending and to Clinton's tax increases. Clinton left office with the Federal Government running a budget surplus.

In foreign affairs, Clinton came close to orchestrating a peace treaty between the Israelis and the Palestinians. However, the Palestinian leader, Yasser Arafat, balked at the last minute and then used a provocation by the right-wing Israeli General Ariel Sharon as an excuse to scuttle the deal and start another violent uprising.

Early in Clinton's Administration, 18 American servicemen died in Somalia. GIs were sent to Somalia by President Bush largely to provide sufficient stability to prevent famine. However, their mission began to morph into supporting the Government against various Somali warlords. When the American troops tried to capture one of these warlords, Somali insurgents trapped them. Had not Pakistani UN forces equipped with tanks broken the Somali siege, the American military may well have endured a disaster equivalent to that of Custer at the Little Big Horn.

After this debacle, Clinton withdrew American forces from Somalia. Conservatives widely denounced this retreat as cowardly, forgetting that President Reagan did much the same thing when terrorists blew up a Marine barracks in Lebanon in 1983, killing 241 Marines.

Unfortunately, Clinton's personal transgressions consumed much of the latter years of his administration. Clinton had been dogged about stories about his womanizing for years. Clinton denied these stories during his campaigns, not completely convincingly. The public was at least willing to believe that whatever sexual escapades he had engaged in prior to becoming president, he would, like Shakespeare's Henry V, behave himself while in office.

Clinton was sued by Paula Jones, who claimed that he had sexually harassed her when Governor of Arkansas. In depositions taken by Jones' lawyers, Clinton denied other affairs or sexual misconduct under oath. Then a former White House intern, Monica Lewinsky, confided in a co-worker about her sexual interaction with Clinton. Kenneth Starr, the Special Prosecutor appointed to investigate other alleged conduct by Clinton and his wife, then pursued the Lewinsky story with a vengeance.

Clinton ended up being impeached by the House of Representatives and barely surviving removal by the Senate. While it is true that the conservatives Republicans were out to get Clinton and never considered his presidency (or that of any Democrat) legitimate, it is also true that Clinton presented his enemies with his head on a platter.

The Presidential Election of 2000

The presidential election of 2000 pitted Clinton's Vice President, Al Gore, estranged from the President by the Lewinsky scandal, against George W. Bush, the Governor of Texas and son of former President George H.W. Bush. The most remarkable facet of this election was that despite receiving more popular votes than Bush, Gore lost the election in the Electoral College. Moreover, those results were highly controversial.

Bush prevailed in the Electoral College by carrying the State of Florida by 537 votes out of almost 6,000,000 that were cast. Bush's victory in the State was aided by confusing ballots and other factors. One of the most important was the third party candidacy of the liberal gadfly Ralph Nader. Nader received 97,000 votes in Florida running as the Green Party candidate. His supporters eschewed Gore because he wasn't Green enough and caused the election of the most hostile president ever to government action to protect the environment. When Nader and his supporters look back on his legacy, they may add to them that he insured that the U.S. Supreme Court and the rest of the federal judiciary would be staffed for the foreseeable future by right-wing conservatives hostile to environmental regulation, consumer protection and everything else that Nader and his supporters favored.

The 2000 election was one of the few featuring the scions of two American political families. Gore was the son of a U.S. Senator and Bush was the grandson of another, in addition to being the son of a former President. Gore's candidacy also represented a trend in which a sitting Vice-President or even the Vice-Presidential candidate on the losing ticket became the heir apparent (Nixon, Humphrey, Edmund Muskie, George H. W. Bush and Gore). This had never been true between the Jefferson and Eisenhower administrations and seems to be a trend abandoned to some extent after 2000. However, the Democratic Vice-Presidential candidates in 2000, Joseph Lieberman, and 2004, John Edwards, harbored presidential ambitions.

The 2000 election was not the first time in American history that the winner of the popular vote lost the election in the Electoral College. It happened in 1876 when Rutherford Hayes was elected over Samuel Tilden and 1888 when the incumbent Democrat Grover Cleveland lost to Benjamin Harrison. After 2000 there was briefly some agitation to eliminate the Electoral College, but the issue quickly died.

Although it was not apparent when George W. Bush was inaugurated on January 20, 2001, he was to govern in a world markedly different than that of his predecessors. This is a world in which American foreign policy is dominated by our relationship to the Islamic world far more than ever before.

Part III: The Twenty First Century: The Age of Oil; Reacquaintance with the Islamic World

Prior to the twentieth century (or least since the end of the Crusades), few in the West knew or cared anything about the people and politics of the Arab world or Iran (Persia). There had been little western interest in any part of the Islamic world since the Turks were defeated at the gates of Vienna in 1683. American interaction with the Arabs was largely limited to combating piracy in the Mediterranean during Jefferson's administration.

The Founding and Spread of Islam

In the sixth century, the spread of Christianity was arrested and to some extent reversed by a new religion, Islam. Mohammad, a young Arab merchant in Mecca, now in Saudi Arabia, claimed to have a revelation from God through the Angel Gabriel in 610. He dictated a new Bible, the Koran, to his followers, who accepted him as the last and greatest prophet of the Devine. Mohammad and his followers quickly subdued other tribes in Arabia and convinced or forced them to convert to his new religion. Within a short time after Mohammad's death in 632, his followers swept across the Middle East and North Africa converting most of the people living in the areas of Muslim conquest, including Christians, Jews and Pagans to Islam.

By 639, the Muslim Arabs had conquered what is now Israel and Egypt. Jerusalem, the holy city of three faiths, remained in Muslim hands until 1917, except for the brief conquest by the Crusaders in the 11th century.

The Muslim conquest extended from India to Spain, which was invaded by Muslims from North Africa in 711. In Europe the Muslim advance was stopped by Charles Martel in France in 732. Beginning in the 10th century, the Christians began reconquering Spain in stages. However, Christian gains in Western Europe were offset by additional Muslim conquests in the East.

The Schism in Islam

It is fairly certain that the number of non-Muslims who knew the difference between a Sunni Muslim and a Shiite Muslim was miniscule prior to the Iranian revolution of 1978-79. The emergence of Iran as a regional power and the war in Iraq have brought the distinction front and center to the Christian West.

Whereas the major schism in Christianity did not occur until the Eastern Church (Orthodox) and the Roman Church split in 1094, Islam had its most important schism very early in its history. One group of Muslims believed that Mohammad's authority was passed down through his family, first to his son-in-law, Ali, and then to his grandson, Hussein. Another group believed that Mohammad's mantle passed to a close associate, chosen by other associates, somewhat like a board of directors operates in choosing a company's Chief Executive Officer.

The leader chosen by the group of associates was proclaimed the Caliph, a position that existed until the Turkish secularist leader Kemal Ataturk abolished it in the 1920s. The caliph's followers are known as Sunni Muslims and constitute far and away the majority of Muslims in the world.

The followers of Ali and Hussein are Shiite Muslims. The most important event in history, other than Muhammad's revelations, for Shiites is the battle of Karbala in 680, when an army of the Sunni Caliph defeated and killed Hussein in what now is Iraq. Another important event is the establishment of Shiite Islam as the state religion of Iran (Persia) in the 16th century. While most Muslims are Sunnis, the Shiites are concentrated in the oil-producing areas of the Persian Gulf. In Iran, they constitute over 95% of the population; in Iraq, they constitute 60%. Shiites also constitute a majority in the eastern oil fields of Sunni-ruled Saudi Arabia, and the small oil-rich sheikdoms of the Persian Gulf, such as Kuwait and Bahrain, as well as in Lebanon.

The rise of the Ottoman Turks

In the 11th century, Turkish tribes from Central Asia, which had adopted Islam, began invading the Christian Byzantine Empire. In the 13th century one of these tribes, the Ottomans established an empire which ultimately extended from present day Iraq to the outskirts of Vienna.

In 1453, the Ottomans, who were Sunnis, conquered Constantinople, the capital of the Eastern Roman Empire. In newly united Spain this heightened the determination of the King Ferdinand and Queen Isabella to drive all non-Christians out of Spain. In 1492, they forced the last Muslim stronghold at Granada to surrender, bringing an end to 777 years of an Islamic political presence in their country.

The Ottomans, however, continued to threaten Europe well into the 17th century. Afterwards, the Ottoman Empire went into decline. The "Young Turks" deposed the Ottoman Sultan in 1908 and then threw their lot in with the Germans in World War I.

Upon the Allied victory in 1918, the British and French dismembered the Ottoman Empire. In its place, they created a number of politically unstable independent states, such as Iraq, Syria, Lebanon and Jordan.

After World War I, Britain also assumed control of the former Ottoman province of Palestine. Jews fleeing persecution by the Russian Czar and then the Nazis returned to the land that had been a Jewish state until destroyed by the Romans two thousand years earlier. They established the State of Israel in 1948 and then fought and have continued to fight the Arabs for control of it.

The West rediscovers the Islamic World

Oil was discovered in Iran in 1908. This brought the area to the attention of the western powers, particularly Great Britain, then the World's most powerful nation due to its domination of the seas. The British were interested in Iran because they needed petroleum for their navy, which was switching from coal to oil as the fuel for its ships. British interests immediately went to Persia to exploit this essential commodity. The discovery of oil in Iraq in 1927, Bahrain in 1932 and Saudi Arabia in 1938 similarly brought western attention to these nations and the Arabs in general.

In the late 1930s Nazi Germany also took an interest in Persian and Iraqi oil. When the Iranian Emperor, or Shah, Reza Pahlavi, became too cozy with the Germans, the British and the Soviets forced him to abdicate in favor of his son, Mohammed Reza Pahlavi. British forces also thwarted a pro-Nazi coup d'etat in Iraq in 1941.

Iranian nationalists led by the Prime Minister Mohammed Mosaddegh became very unhappy with Iran's share of the revenue generated by its oil industry. Mosaddegh attempted to nationalize the Anglo-Persian Oil Company. The Shah, pressured by the British, opposed Mosaddegh, but was forced to flee his country. However, in 1953 the British and the American Central Intelligence Agency engineered a coup that returned to Shah to power and ended the Mosaddegh's political career. The coup, however, created simmering anger towards the West among many Iranians.

The Fall of the Shah of Iran

The Shah remained America's most important ally in the Middle East until he was overthrown in January 1979. Up until late 1978, he appeared to be solidly in control of his country. Underneath the surface, however, opposition to the Shah was growing. It was led by an aged cleric, Ayatollah Ruhollah Khomeini. When the Shah persuaded Iraq's dictator Saddam Hussein to expel Khomeini, who had been living in Iraq for years, the Ayatollah went to Paris, where he rallied the Shah's opponents behind him and soon created the conditions that led to the collapse of the Shah's regime.

Upon the fall of the Shah, Khomeini established the Islamic Republic of Iran, an anti-western theocratic state. This event is a turning point in history every bit as significant as the outbreak of World War I, the Communist seizure of power in Russia, or indeed the fall of the Soviet Union and the end of the Cold War.

The Iran-Iraq War 1980-88

That the Iranian Revolution did not have immediate impact on the West (other than Iran's holding the American embassy staff hostage for 444 days from November 1979 to January 1981) was due to the invasion of Iran by the Iraqi dictator Saddam Hussein. Overlooked at the time President George Bush decided to go to war and force Saddam out of power in 2003, was the fact that in the 1980's Saddam was somewhat of an ally of the United States in keeping the Iranians at bay.

However, by 1988, both Iran and Iraq were bled white and they signed a peace accord. Saddam's attention then turned to his small oil-rich neighbor, Kuwait, which Iraqis considered to be part of their country. The West, however, was not about to give Saddam control of such a large share of the Middle East's oil. In January 1991, a coalition of western and Arab nations destroyed much of Saddam's army and forced him to evacuate Kuwait.

The United States also established a "no-fly zone" in the northern Iraq, creating an essentially independent Kurdish state in that part of the country. The Kurds are a non-Arab Muslim people living primarily in Iraq, Iran and Eastern Turkey. They have been at odds with the governments of all three countries, particularly Turkey, where Kurdish separatists have waged a bloody rebellion against the Turkish state. The Kurds in Iraq live in one of the most oil-abundant regions of the country.

However, at the end of the Gulf War the Shiite majority of Iraq was left to the tender mercies of Saddam Hussein, who was as brutal a thug as any who ever ruled a nation. During his reign of terror, Saddam used poison gas against the Iranians and rebellious Kurds in his own country, as well as frequently resorting to torture and murder to maintain control of his nation. Saddam's sons were as brutal as their father, frequently raping Iraqi women who caught their fancy.

Al-Qaida

One of the main concerns of the United States in forcing Saddam Hussein out of Kuwait was the security of Saudi Arabia, the major supplier of American oil imports. The U.S. sent troops to Saudi Arabia to protect it from Saddam and as a staging area for operations against Iraq. After the Gulf War ended, American troops stayed on Saudi soil.

The presence of non-Muslim troops in Saudi Arabia, home to the holiest of Muslim sites, Mecca and Medina, greatly angered many pious Muslims. Among those was a Saudi citizen named Osama Bin Laden, who had joined the Islamists' fight against the Soviet puppet government of Afghanistan. Bin Laden founded the group called Al-Qaida ("the base" in English), which turned its attention to driving the United States and other non-Muslims out of Saudi Arabia and other Muslim countries after the Russians evacuated Afghanistan in 1989.

Al-Qaida attacks the United States

In the 1990s, Al-Qaida launched several attacks on American institutions and personnel in the Middle East and Africa. It blew up the American embassy in Kenya, killing more than 200 people in 1998 and attacked an American Navy ship, the U.S.S. Cole at port in Yemen in 2000, killing 14 American sailors and wounding many others.

George W. Bush's first term: The September 11 attack and America's response

On September 11, 2001, about eight months into the presidency of George W. Bush, 19 members of Al-Qaida, mostly Saudi citizens, hijacked four domestic airliners. Two were flown into the World Trade Center towers in New York, killing almost 3,000 people, One was flown into the Pentagon in Arlington, Virginia, killing about 200 and the fourth crashed in Pennsylvania, killing all aboard.

George W. Bush entered the White House with some very specific goals. First on his list of things was to do was finish off FDR's New Deal by starving domestic programs with military spending and tax cuts. His second objective was to depose Saddam Hussein. Bush believed his father had made a mistake by letting Saddam remain in power and he was also motivated by Saddam's attempt to assassinate his father during the 1990s.

The September 11 attacks produced a spike in the President's popularity that gave him a carte blanche to do virtually anything he desired. Instead of using it as a tool to unify the American people, Bush put the tragedy to work as a political tool. He also seized upon it as an excuse to depose Saddam Hussein.

The Bush Administration concocted a link between Saddam and the September 11 attacks where none existed. Secondly, it fabricated evidence as to the dangers Saddam posed to the United States. It did this most notably by suggesting that the Iraqi dictator was acquiring the means to build nuclear weapons from Africa, as well as stockpiling chemical and biological weapons. Since Saddam had used poison gas against the Iranians and Kurds in the 1980s, there was no reason to think he wouldn't use it again.

Bush's first response to the September 11 attacks was to demand that the Taliban government of Afghanistan turn over Osama Bin Laden and other Al-Qaida leaders, who were living in Afghanistan. The Taliban, an extremist Sunni religious group, refused to do so. Bush launched military operations against the Afghan regime. However, because Bush was laying the groundwork to attack Iraq as well, the commitment of forces to Afghanistan was far too small to capture Bin Laden and the Al-Qaida leadership.

Although the United States was successful in initially deposing the Taliban government, the movement has regrouped and as of 2012 is prevented from retaking control of Afghanistan only by the presence of the 100,000 plus American troops in that country. When Barack Obama became President in 2009, he markedly reduced the number of American soldiers in Iraq and markedly increased the number in Afghanistan. It remains to be seen whether either move makes any difference in the future of either country.

Bush began laying the groundwork for attacking Iraq soon after the September 11 attacks and demanded that Saddam come clean and either prove that he did not have "weapons of mass destruction" or rid Iraq of such weapons. As it turned out, Saddam didn't have such weapons and in retrospect many Americans could not understand why he simply didn't allow sufficient inspections to prove this. However, Saddam could not let the Iranians know that Iraq was virtually defenseless. With a population that was 60 % Shiite, Saddam would have been inviting an attack from Shiite Iran.

While there were some vocal opponents to Bush's drumbeat for war, most American politicians were afraid to stand in his way, particularly those running for re-election in 2002. The most notable exception was Senator Paul Wellstone of Minnesota, the only Democrat running for re-election actively opposing Bush's push towards war with Iraq. Wellstone, his wife and daughter were killed in an airplane crash shortly before the election. It is most likely that had he lived he would have been rewarded for his political courage by being defeated at the polls. His stand-in, former Vice-President Walter Mondale, was defeated by Republican Norman Coleman.

The American assault on Iraq began on March 19, 2003 and quickly routed and destroyed Saddam Hussein's Army. Bush's popularity skyrocketed and he played it up to the hilt by landing on an aircraft carrier in May 2003 and declaring "Mission Accomplished." However, the practicalities of establishing a stable, secure government to replace Saddam soon took the shine off the euphoria from America's initial success.

First of all, remnants of Saddam's military and Sunni and Shiite extremists (or nationalists, depending on your point of view) began waging a guerrilla war against American forces, killing many more GIs than died during the conventional war with Saddam. The insurgents relied on roadside bombs and occasional suicide bombers to wreck havoc upon American troops and the government. Iraq descended into chaos.

Meanwhile, the Sunni minority, which had ruled Iraq since time immemorial, had no intention of handing the country over to the Shiite majority and a quasi civil war broke out between the two sects. Many Shiites also were less than grateful to the Americans for delivering them from Saddam. Muqtada al-Sadr, a fiery young Shiite cleric, demanded that the Americans leave Iraq and initiated a bloody insurgency against U.S. troops and the forces of the interim Iraqi government. Al-Sadr's ultimate goal is a theocratic Shiite state similar to and closely allied with the Islamic Republic of Iran.

At this point, the results of the American War in Iraq can be summarized as follows: 1) We succeeded in deposing (and ultimately capturing) Saddam Hussein, an incredibly brutal dictator, who the Iraqi Government executed. 2) We left Iraq an unstable country politically and left certain Iraqi minorities, particularly the Christian community, in a worse situation than existed under Saddam. 3) We greatly enhanced the power of the Islamic Republic of Iran by removing the greatest counterweight to its regional and global ambitions--Saddam Hussein.

Bush's second term

By the time of the 2004 election it was readily apparent that the Iraq War was not the unqualified success that Bush and his Defense Secretary, Donald Rumsfeld, promised. Moreover, the Bush tax cuts did not produce the economic growth he and his advisors predicted. What they did produce a growing Federal budget deficit. Vice President Richard Cheney stated that deficits do not matter, a proposition that the Republican Party quickly abandoned when Barack Obama became President and wanted to spend federal money to combat the recession that began late in Bush's second term.

Despite diminishing popularity, Bush was narrowly re-elected in 2004. A curious aspect of the election campaign was the reopening of the animosities festering about the denouement of the Vietnam War. Right-wing conservatives, including many veterans, launched a concerted attack on the war record of the Democratic candidate, Senator John Kerry of Massachusetts. Details of Kerry's service, who in fact had seen combat in Vietnam, became more of an issue than Bush's avoidance of Vietnam service by joining the Texas National Air Guard. Kerry's real crime to the political right was his leadership role in the anti-war movement when he returned from Vietnam, for which the political right will never forgive him.

Bush's popularity diminished even more when the Federal Government completely mishandled the flooding of New Orleans in the aftermath of Hurricane Katrina in August 2005. Due to this and his proposals to privatize Social Security, the Democrats won back control of the Congress in 2006.

At the end of 2007, the longest post-war recession in the United States began and in 2008 the financial system of the United States almost collapsed due in part to the risky loans by American investment banks. Most of these loans were tied to the marked increase in housing prices during the Bush presidency. By late 2007 many mortgagees began to default on these loans, the housing price bubble burst and investment banks discovered that many of their financial instruments were worthless.

In late 2008, the Bush Administration realized that government intervention was necessary to prevent a complete meltdown of the American financial system and to some extent abandoned its free market mantra. It used Government funds to buy assets and make loans to save a number of large American corporations and investments banks, such as the investment bank Bear Stearns and American International Group, the largest insurance company in the United States. These companies were deemed by the Government to be "too big to fail." The Obama Administration continued this policy.

Barack Obama

Barack Obama was born in 1961 in Hawaii to a Caucasian mother and a Kenyan graduate student father. Some of his detractors, known as "birthers" insist that he was born in Kenya and thus ineligible to be President, since the Constitution requires that the President be a natural born U.S. citizen. The "birthers" have not a shred of evidence to support their theory, which is motivated by their desire to delegitimize any Democratic candidate.

At the time of Obama's birth, the racist vestige of slavery, the Civil War and the southern reaction to emancipation was so pronounced that the marriage of his parents would have been illegal in a number of states. The violence against blacks in Birmingham and Selma, Alabama, the slayings of the civil rights workers in Mississippi and other racist violence was still in the future. The idea that a half African boy would grow up to be President was absolutely preposterous.

Obama's political career was equally astounding and meteoric. As a state senator and candidate for the U.S. Senate, Obama was selected to give the keynote address at the 2004 Democratic convention. This made him a national figure. He was easily elected to the U.S. Senate from Illinois in 2004, blessed by incredible good fortune. The Republican incumbent chose not to run for re-election. His Democratic predecessor chose not to run for the seat. The winner of the Republican primary withdrew his candidacy and Obama faced the Republican African-American gadfly, Alan Keyes, in the general election. Obama won 70% of the vote against what was in actuality token opposition.

The presumptive Democratic candidate for the presidency in 2008 was Hillary Clinton, wife of the ex-President, then a Senator from New York. However, there were elements in the party uncomfortable with Hillary, in part due to the fear that the scandals, real and alleged from the Clinton presidency and Arkansas years, would emerge again in the 2008 campaign. Obama became the alternative to a Hillary Clinton candidacy.

After winning the Democratic nomination, Obama was aided in the general election by a terrible economic climate. He was also helped by his opponent, Arizona Senator John McCain, a Vietnam War hero who had spent six years as a prisoner in North Vietnam after his plane was shot down over Hanoi. McCain, knowing that he had an uphill battle in light of the recession that began in late 2007, and knowing that he was not entirely trusted by the far right of the Republican party, chose as his running mate, Alaska Governor Sarah Palin. Palin quickly demonstrated that she was totally unfit to be President. That she could become President if McCain was elected was a distinct possibility given McCain's age, 72, and his history of skin cancer.

As President, Obama quickly changed the emphasis of U.S. military activity in the Middle East from Iraq to Afghanistan. After three years, however, it appears doubtful that the government in either country can survive without American troops. His greatest foreign policy triumph (for which his detractors deny him any credit) was the finding and killing of Osama Bin Laden, the mastermind of the September 11, 2001 attacks, by U.S. Navy Seals in Pakistan on May 2, 2011.

That Obama deserves credit for authorizing the Seals' raid on Bin Laden's compound should be obvious from what would have happened had the mission failed. He was taking a huge risk. Had the mission failed and had American servicemen been killed in the operation, Obama would have been castigated as was President Carter when he authorized the ill-fated mission to rescue American hostages in 1980. Given the vitriol directed towards him, it is likely that his detractors would have suggested that he intended the mission to fail.

Economic policies

Obama attacked the recession by increasing federal government spending in the hope that it would stimulate an economic recovery. He continued to loan government money and buy the assets of major corporations to prevent their collapse. The beneficiaries of this policy included General Motors and CitiCorp.

Since Obama took office, stock prices have recovered to some extent from their lows in early 2008, but as of early 2012, there had been little improvement in the unemployment rate, which remained over 9%. Liberal economists fault Obama for spending too little federal money to stimulate the economy. The Republicans insist that tax cuts will spur investment and pull the United States out of the recession.

The Health Care Law

Health insurance for every American has been a goal of every Democratic President since Truman. Republicans have heretofore successfully combated every effort in this regard. When the Clinton Administration proposed universal health insurance, the Republicans and the private health insurance industry waged such a successful campaign against it, that they not only killed the initiative, but won control of the Congress in 1994.

Obama succeeded in getting the first universal health insurance law passed in his first term. The Republicans now are using every conceivable strategy; lawsuit and budgetary maneuvers to kill this legislation. It is obvious that changes in the American health care system are long overdue. Individuals without health insurance are presented with bills that they cannot possibly pay. Any person seeking to change jobs must be very careful not to lose health insurance coverage in doing so.

The upshot of the present system is that either those without medical insurance and their families do not get the care they need, or the rest of society ends up paying for their care in some manner. Thus, the insured either pay higher medical insurance premiums or see the cost of care for the uninsured hidden in their own medical bills.

The cost of health care in the United States has risen dramatically. This is due to numerous factors. One is the advent of new and very expensive technology. Another is the graying of the American population. People are living longer and now need treatment for conditions which they previously would not lived long enough to acquire, or which would have killed them in short order.

Where do we go from here?

Unlike certain periods of the past, such as during the Vietnam era, there is little difference between the major American political parties on issues concerning defense and foreign affairs. Both parties are preoccupied with insuring American access to sufficient quantities of petroleum at an acceptable price. This may prove to be more difficult than before given the political upheavals in the Middle East and Iran's determination to acquire nuclear weapons and become a world power.

With regard to domestic issues, the American people will be able to choose between two very different visions of their country in November 2012. The Republican vision is of a country where anyone with any pluck can make themselves comfortable, if not wealthy, by the sweat of their brow. The Democratic vision is one in which a good share of society's resources must be allocated to provide a basic standard of living to the unproductive and underproductive members of American society.

Subsidizing the unproductive does not mean simply giving money to the lazy. It also requires support of the children of poorer families, the elderly, the truly disabled and the unlucky. This requires a redistribution of wealth through the tax system.

Prior to the Great Depression, and more recently since Ronald Reagan, it has been the Republican vision that has predominated. The Democrats contend that the increasing inequality of wealth in this country has created a social crisis. The next election may depend on how many voters who agree with them bother to show up at the polls.

AUTHOR'S NOTE AND BIO

I have been reading history books for fifty-five years, starting, I believe, with *Nuremberg Diary* by the American Prison Psychologist, G. M. Gilbert. In writing this book I have refreshed my recollections by consulting various sources. I reread for example, all three volumes of Samuel Eliot Morison's *Oxford History of the United States* and James McPherson's *Battle Cry of Freedom: The Civil War Era.* I have also relied on the research I did for my prior books:

> ***Killed In Action: The life and times of SP4 Stephen H. Warner, draftee, journalist and anti-war activist,*** a history of the Vietnam War told through the life of an anti-war draftee who was killed in action in 1971; ***The Most Famous Soldier in America,*** a biography of Nelson Miles, a Civil War and Indian Wars hero; The ***Kaiser's Senator,*** a book about Senator Bob LaFollette and the anti-war movement in World War I; ***Heroes, Martyrs and Survivors of the Civil War,*** a book of biographical sketches of 22 Civil War figures.

I graduated magna cum laude from Miami University, Oxford, Ohio in 1967 and from Harvard Law School in 1972. I was drafted into the United States Army in 1969 and was stationed in Saigon, South Vietnam from April 1970 to March 1971. My professional career had been as a government attorney and administrative law judge in labor relations and related fields.

Made in the USA
Middletown, DE
04 June 2024

55237235R00089